MARKETING ACROSS THE GENERATIONS

FIFTY-PLUS

Produced by the Center for Professional Development,
CUNA & Affiliates, Madison, Wisconsin,
in cooperation with MEMBERS Prime Club.

MEMBERS Prime Club is a nonprofit organization affiliated with
the Credit Union National Association, CUNA Mutual Group,
and individual credit unions. Members receive special savings, discounts,
and services. Membership is open to present or former U.S. credit union members
age 50-plus or retired. For more information on MEMBERS Prime Club, visit
http://www.cunamutual.com/custaff/membserv.asp
or e-mail: mpc@cunamutual.com.

Product #22897

Sarah White

CUNA & Affiliates

KENDALL/HUNT PUBLISHING COMPANY
4050 Westmark Drive   Dubuque, Iowa 52002

Written by Sarah White
Developmental edit by Joan Donovan
Produced by Beth Stetenfeld
Production assistance by Elaine Harrop and Rachel Imsland

Copyright © 2000
Credit Union National Association, Inc.

ISBN 0-7872-6908-5

Printed in the United States of America
10 9 8 7 6 5 4 3 2 1

CONTENTS

ACKNOWLEDGMENTS

My thanks to these credit union marketers from around the country who shared their insights and experiences in marketing to matures:

Amy Crowe, CUNA Credit Union; Darlene Diamond, Energy First Credit Union; Joe Hearn, Dupaco Community Credit Union; Jeff York, Vista Federal Credit Union; Donna Zaccour, Seaboard Credit Union.

Thanks also to the handbook reviewers: Donna Bellows, North Country Credit Union; Nevada Bovee, Northern Schools Federal Credit Union; Jill Grushon-Maeder, Universal 1 Credit Union; Nancy Layton, Service Credit Union; and Phil Tschudy, MEMBERS Prime Club.

I'd also like to thank the staff of CUNA's Center for Professional Development, especially Jim Jerving, for general support in the production of this handbook. I also appreciate the help of Jack Fererri and Joan Donovan in expanding my thinking.

ABOUT THE AUTHOR

Sarah White is a freelance writer and advertising consultant based in Madison, Wisconsin. For more information about the author visit her web site at *http://userpages.chorus.net/whites.*

INTRODUCTION

The generational cohort to which a member belongs is a significant factor affecting perceptions of "the good life"—from what we consider financial security to which musical styles we prefer. The *Marketing Across the Generations* series consists of four books that help credit unions develop marketing programs based on segmentation by generational cohort. It's a new way of looking at customer segments, based on the shared life experiences that create bonds among members of a generation.

Labels like "generation X" and "the baby boom" are familiar expressions. *Marketing Across the Generations: Fifty-Plus* identifies distinct generational segments within the 50-plus population. These groups are discussed as "primes," ages 50–64, "seniors," ages 65–79, and "elders," ages 80–plus. Key characteristics make each of these three segments unique. To serve our members, we must look beyond our stereotypes of "old age" to develop insightful products, services, and messages appropriate to these unique segments within the mature market.

Credit union marketers are realizing that soon, more of the U.S. population will be over than under age 50. Today's 50-plus market already accounts for a large majority of the personal wealth in financial institutions. The mindset of many of these matures is a natural match with the credit union philosophy. Their values of loyalty, conservatism, and service have become values of the credit union movement itself. The credit union brand holds great appeal for this large demographic segment.

This book is designed to help you create programs and services that better serve the needs of your current and prospective members over age 50.

WHAT'S COVERED

Chapters discuss strategic planning, media usage, retail marketing, and suggestions for creating marketing materials that matures respond to. Each chapter ends with "Credit Union Action Steps," designed to help you move from big ideas to specific practical action.

Chapter 1 explains market segmentation by generational cohorts, defining terms for subsets within the mature market.

Chapter 2 describes older members' importance to credit unions. This segment has been aggressively marketed to by banks, while remaining largely underserved by credit unions, resulting in significant attrition. Successful credit unions will buck this trend. Serving the older member means meeting their needs for loans, financial advice, and deposit products.

Chapter 3 focuses on the strategic marketing process for the mature market. A review of the strategic marketing process—from determining mission through SWOT analysis, choosing strategies, preparing an action plan, and evaluating performance—brings the inexperienced marketer up to speed. The importance of research to understand members aged 50+ is emphasized. The objective of our marketing is one-to-one relationships that last a lifetime.

Chapter 4 guides the reader in creating a step-by-step marketing plan addressing the mature market. Two credit unions' mature market programs provide in-depth examples.

Chapter 5 explores mature market promotional programs and media strategies. Three scenarios of credit union mature market programs are evaluated. Mass media and other approaches to communicating with this market are discussed.

Chapter 6 discusses retail marketing choices that augment the experience of older members visiting the credit union. Emerging practices, such as the use of concierges and supertellers, are described. The chapter emphasizes empathy and communication skills for member-contact staff, as well as physical design issues such as security and accessibility.

Chapter 7 moves the discussion to leveraging existing mature market programs for greater results. Ideas for marketing materials, using the Internet, and designing an outstanding activities club are offered. The chapter ends with a look at the future of the mature market and recommendations for serving tomorrow's fifty-plus member.

HOW TO USE THIS HANDBOOK

The books in the *Marketing Across the Generations* series are directed to marketing staff and management, senior management, and directors in credit unions. Different readers will find the books useful in different ways.

If you are a member of senior management, you will find vision here that will help you understand the motivations, desires, and needs of your member base. In the past, credit unions have done a poor job of serving older members. This group remains underserved, even though the mature market possesses enormous economic resources, and is growing in numbers. Attracting and serving these members is vital to the long-term stability of credit unions. In *Marketing Across the Generations: Fifty-Plus* you'll find inspiration and actionable insights to reshape your relationship with mature members.

Everyone in the credit union is responsible for delivering great member service, to every member, young or old. If you work in a management role, you need to be sure the entire credit union staff understands generational marketing. This book contains suggestions for training frontline staff, and for improving aspects of your physical environment, to better serve older members.

If you are in a marketing position, you will find specific strategies, case studies, and examples of creative approaches that will help you build a powerful mature market program. We've included step-by-step instructions on building a basic program, for those relatively new to the marketing process, and many idea-starters for veteran marketers who want to expand existing programs.

Use this handbook as you like. Browse it, share it with managers and staff, follow the Action Steps that guide you toward your own unique program. Some concepts may spark conversation among your peers. Consider holding a discussion group, after several of you have finished reading.

We've drawn examples from credit unions around the country. We've sought inspiration among the work of futurists, demographers, and sociologists. The combination moves the "cutting edge" of credit union marketing into the twenty-first century.

GENERATIONAL MARKETING

"The marketplace is an economy built on dreams.
These dreams of consumers have their own vernacular,
and signal various badges and connections . . .
[They] are the aspirations that open up opportunities
for the savvy marketer, and generation is a big part
of understanding the aspirations."

— *J. Walker Smith and Ann Clurman,* Public Perspective

Call to mind your last annual meeting.

Visualize the auditorium or banquet hall—the podium at the front, the room filled with members, executives, and staff. Think about the faces of the members in the room that night: young and old and in between. Who are these people? What do you really know about them?

You know that some of those members are profitable to serve; others, less so. You know that some of them are proud of their affiliation with their credit union. They frequently refer new individuals for membership. They open accounts for their relatives, sharing the benefits of credit union membership with their loved ones.

If you could focus on the most profitable, most supportive members in that audience, who would they be? If you could put them to work for you as a sales force, what impact might they have on your bottom line? If I then told you that the most productive and profitable members of your sales force were often considered "over the hill" by society at large, would you question that label? Probably. But you would agree that those productive and profitable members share characteristics in common that make them identifiable as a specific segment of your membership. One of those characteristics is likely to be their age.

Credit Union Marketing Is Changing

As a credit union marketer, you likely direct much of your effort toward targeting specific segments of current or potential membership for special promotions, products, and services. There is good reason to do so, as past experience has shown.

We cannot, however, maximize our future opportunities by repeating our past successes. The *Marketing Across the Generations* series provides a new way of looking at customer segments, drawing on recent demographic and sociological research. Generational marketing focuses on psychological characteristics shared by those of a specific age cohort. Phrases like "born at the right time" capture the feel of generational marketing. The basic insight—that our generational cohort is highly predictive of who we are, what we believe, and how we buy—is proving correct. Marketers across the United States are applying this thinking to advertising campaigns, product design, and all the other activities of marketing, with great success.

Our generational cohort is highly predictive of who we are, what we believe, and how we buy.

Credit union marketers are becoming increasingly sophisticated. We may once have believed "marketing is what you do until you have enough members," but no longer. We are establishing credit unions as strong financial services brands, steeped in the values of community, cooperation, and service.

A Refresher: Why We Study Markets by Segments

Not everyone will buy your product or service. But some segment of them will, and those who do can be identified by traits they share—traits like geographic location, demographic profile, and lifestyle. When we attempt to identify what traits buyers have in common, that is called *market segmentation*. When we base a

---

marketing strategy on our knowledge of that segment, it is called a *target marketing strategy,* or another way of saying the same thing, a *market segmentation strategy.*

The premise of this book (and the others in the *Marketing Across the Generations* series) is that market segmentation based on generational cohorts is an effective strategy for credit unions. To support that premise, let's fill in the background.

When we pursue a target marketing strategy, we look for the collection of traits that will allow us to predict the ways that group will behave. We know the segment we have targeted will be likely to respond in a similar way to a specific product offering, or marketing message. The key is to understand who is responding to what, and why, so we can use that knowledge to design product/service offerings and marketing messages that fit the targeted market segment like a glove.

Permission to Skim This Section

If you read "Hardy Boys" or "Nancy Drew" mysteries as a youth, you know each book started with a chapter describing the circumstances that produced these child detectives. You probably skipped chapter one after the first few novels—you already knew what it had to say.

If you have a strong marketing background, and are familiar with the rationale for market segmentation strategies, feel free to skim this chapter. Note that we don't say "skip"—there is new terminology and new thinking here you will want to familiarize yourself with, before moving on to other chapters.

If you are relatively new to marketing, or want a refresher, read on. The background in this chapter will help you assimilate the new insights in later chapters.

From Mass Market to Millennium. Fifty years ago, America was well on its way to being the mass consumer society depicted in beloved old situation comedies like "I Love Lucy" and "The Dick Van Dyke Show." The families gathering in living rooms around a flickering TV set to watch those shows were a consumer group so broad and general in scope, they were defined by nothing more than their ability to purchase an offering. Marketers didn't trouble with descriptors such as geographic location, age, gender, or cultural background. They simply offered products to viewers, who, with their postwar purchasing power, aspired to the dreams the sitcom characters depicted. These consumers bought the soap powders, canned soups, and washing machines shown in the programs and the commercials, and knew they were gaining on the good life by doing so. Some of those consumers bought homes, financed cars, and educated children through a relatively new consumer movement: the credit union.

Fast-forward fifty years. Today, the mass market is a thing of the past. We're a nation dividing itself into smaller and smaller subcategories. We want products and services that fit our specific needs, not those of a large mass of people who may be nothing like us. Today, marketers look for segments with specific attributes, as a tool to focus both energy and spending. We want to spend our dollars reaching the potential members most likely to buy our products and services.

We want products and services that fit our specific needs, not those of a large mass of people.

While we can't very well develop a specific product for each unique customer, by segmenting the market and designing products, services, and messages to appeal to those segments, we come closer to reaching individuals in ways that match their unique needs and desires.

Slice and Serve. The segmentation process always starts with geography—within what region will we be looking for customers? Then, we proceed to classify inhabitants of that region by a variety of other attributes, depending on our purposes. We might look at demographics—age, race, family type—or spending habits, media preferences, and lifestyles. If they are currently customers, we look at their previous purchase patterns. By classifying the market and analyzing the segments, we can determine potentially profitable segments.

To qualify as "potentially profitable," a market segment must include enough individuals to achieve reasonable economies of scale; and the segment must be unique enough in its characteristics that we can easily identify who is and who isn't in the group.

Target marketing is not without its downside. There are costs associated with the move from mass market to separate niches. There may be higher research costs, as you study each market segment in detail. There may be separate marketing strategies to execute—maybe even separate products, or packages of products, to

---

develop for each segment. Different distribution channels may be required to meet the needs of different segments—home financial services for some, new drive-throughs for others, sit-down member consulting areas for still others. The efficiency of "one size fits all" disappears in a network of market segmentation strategies.

Then why should credit unions pursue segmentation? Because—bottom line—it results in better relationships with members. By tailoring what you offer to meet your members' needs, and tailoring how you communicate to how they like to be approached, you become the credit union of their dreams. That's a competitive position that's hard to beat.

AGES, STAGES, AND COHORTS

There is power in examining your membership by generational cohort. Where members have needs for tailored products and services, there exist nonmembers with similar needs who could be added to your roster.

J. Walker Smith and Ann Clurman propose in *Rocking the Ages, The Yankelovich Report on Generational Marketing* that, "Members of a generation are linked through the shared life experiences of their formative years." It's a simple thought, and a powerful one. Experiences create bonds that tie members of a generation together. Contrast the reunions of Dunkirk Invasion survivors on the one hand, and Woodstock Music Festival veterans on the other, to sense the emotional power summoned by generational bonds built on experiences.

These shared experiences inform the values and skills of each group as they go through life. Social scientists refer to these generational groups as *cohorts*. The shared values and experiences of a cohort provide the lens through which that group views life. The generational cohort we belong to is a significant factor in our individual conception of "the good life," affecting everything from what we consider financial security to what music we prefer to listen to.

For the purposes of the *Marketing Across the Generations* series, at the beginning of the 21st century, we generally define four "peer generations" with potential for credit unions interested in segmentation strategies:

- Youth (0–19)
- Generation X (20–35)

- Baby Boomers (35–53)
- Matures (50 and above)

It is, of course, a fallacy to state authoritatively that one generation ends and the next begins on the eve of a new year. The generational cohorts are not, after all, four candy bars moving along life's assembly line—a better metaphor would be a multitude of small candies scattered all over the factory.

Baby Boomers: Old? Many of the leading demographic researchers, including the Yankelovich firm, and Age Wave Communications, make a practice of including the oldest baby boomers (those 50 or older) in the category of "matures"—labeling everyone born before 1950 the "mature market." Whether those 50- to 55-year-olds really think and feel like part of the "mature market" is debatable. If they have gained financial success, they are likely dealing with mature life stage issues: planning for retirement, refining investment strategies, enjoying increased leisure and family time. For these individuals, financial products geared toward the needs of older people are appropriate. However, the marketing message had better not address them as "old" or even as "seniors"!

Those 50- to 55-year-olds whose careers have produced relatively less wealth are still living lives hemmed in by baby boom concerns. These individuals are balancing work and family, paying off loans, and struggling to "graduate" from borrower to saver status. It's important to recognize that not all 50- to 55-year-olds have the same priorities.

The 50-plus population is as diverse as the under-50 population.

Diversity in Maturity. While most credit unions use age 50 as the generational "floor" for mature marketing strategies, bear in mind that we are dealing with a whole spectrum of individuals who may vary considerably from the stereotypical "senior citizen." Many financial marketers make the mistake of viewing people 50 and older as one mass market. Actually, the 50-plus population is as diverse as the under-50 population. The needs of an actively employed 52-year-old are quite different from those of a 72-year-old retiree. Even two mature individuals of the same age may have very different needs, depending on each individual's health, income, and other factors.

What to Call Them?

Much has been written about mature market segmentation, and almost none of it refers to this group as "seniors." Various nicknames have been invented, from "Silvers" to "Chronologically Enhanced." For simplicity's sake we have chosen to use the term "mature" or "mature market" when referring to everyone over age 50. However, to break down this large market into manageable subgroups, we will use age, life stage, and generational factors—then offer simple working labels for easy identification.

We'll begin by dividing the over-50 market into three age segments, which we'll call middle adults (50–64), late adults (65–79), and elders (80-plus.) Each segment has predictable concerns that make it unique and discreet from the others.

Age Distinctions. Age remains the easiest way to discuss the segments within the mature market. Segmenting markets based on ages is not new. Particular needs and desires can be associated with particular ages. Most eighteen-year-olds want a car, a checkbook, and an education. Most young families want to purchase a home. As those families mature, their needs evolve through predictable patterns of financial needs. Marketers have been leveraging these observations for some time.

Life Stages

Until very recently, life stages were practically inseparable from chronological age. Lives followed a predictable, linear course: birth, education, marriage, work, childrearing, and perhaps a brief retirement, ending in death. No longer. Today the average age of retirement has dropped to 62 while average life expectancy is close to 80 years. Older adults are healthier and more financially stable. As a result, we are today seeing possibilities for a variety of life stages and defining experiences that aren't good predictors of a person's age. We see second families, second careers, second educations. Life is becoming a cyclical affair, with periods of education, work, and leisure recurring at various times.

---

*Life is becoming a cyclical affair, with periods of
education, work, and leisure recurring at various times.*

Age Wave Communications defines life stages as "milestones in a person's life when the normal course of events is substantially altered and the *most significant relationships in our life often change*." As we make the transition from one phase to another, our needs change on many levels. We often rearrange our physical world to accommodate our new life stage. We may move from a larger home to an apartment; or move in the other direction, if starting a second family. The implications for financial service institutions are not hard to see. Home improvement loans, mortgages, and estate planning are just a few of the products for which a transition in life stage creates a need.

Age Wave has identified several life stages that can occur in our mature years:

- *Empty nesting.* Individuals and couples have more time, more money, and a renewed sense of freedom and vitality than they have known while raising children. Leisure activities and personal fulfillment become new priorities. These people are likely to be dynamic midlifers.

- *Caregiving.* Many individuals over 50 have continued responsibility for caregiving, whether for children, grandchildren, or elderly parents and relatives. Often referred to as the "sandwich generation," these individuals are squeezed by the needs of others. Their experience of life is more frenzied than they would like. Time for self, and money-saving activities, become important.

- *Grandparenthood.* Older individuals who are healthy and financially secure are using their extra time and money to nurture relationships with grandchildren— relationships that will last much longer than in the past, due to the increase in life expectancy. Credit unions help that relationship by promoting paired activities between their senior clubs and youth clubs.

- *Singlehood.* Many older adults experience singlehood through divorce, widowhood, or simply never having married. Since life expectancy for men is somewhat shorter than for women, many of these single people are female. This life stage brings a renewed interest in social activities, which sometimes lead to dating and remarriage.

- *Retirement.* Many individuals are now experiencing twenty to twenty-five years of retirement. Couples may actually spend more time together as a couple in retirement than they did as parents of a family. They may devote some of that time to travel, volunteer activities, and education for the simple joy of learning. Good health care and solid financial planning are the keys to making these years rewarding.

One or more of these life stages could be taking place for a prime, a senior, or an elder. It could be met with the unique personality traits of a baby boomer, a silent, or a member of the G.I. generation. If you have trouble accepting this, just consider: well-known actor Ed Asner was born in 1929, has a son born in 1987, and a wife whom he married in 1998. (That makes him a senior, "silent," nonretired parent recovering from singlehood!)

The Generational Difference. Each segment has been imprinted with a unique identity, courtesy of the moment in time in which it came of age. Common experiences in the young-adult years shape values and preferences that persist over a lifetime. These experiences—a mix of historical, economic, political, and cultural influences—bind a group together in a cohort identity. This is not to say all members feel identically about all issues. Just ask a roomful of 50-year-olds whether they supported the Vietnam War, if you want to see diversity of opinion. There will always be people who fall far from the normative middle on any given dimension of behavior or belief. But statistics tell us that the majority will fall toward the center—and therein lies the efficiency of generational marketing.

Generational marketing teaches us that different generations are likely to react differently as they reach the same chronological stages. For this reason, we cannot simply think of the 50-plus market as consisting of middle adults, late adults, and elders. The unique individuals who today qualify as middle adults will carry their uniqueness forward as they age. While their needs may change from those associated with the middle-adult years to those of late adults and eventually elders, *the way they approach these needs* will be true to their generational identity, sometimes called "peer personality."

"What to Call Them?"—Revisited

Key characteristics mark each of the three cohorts within your membership who are over age 50. Their chronological age identifies them as middle adults, late adults, and elders. But as distinct market subsegments, they need their own labels. We propose the following.

"Primes" (middle adults ages 50–64)

Primes are middle adults in their peak earning years. Born, for the most part, between 1936 and 1953, they have participated fully in the middle-class American Dream. The youngest—those born between 1946 and 1950—represent the leading edge of the baby boomers. These "aging" boomers are gradually assuming pre-retirement concerns. Primes tend to be materialistic, spiritual in conventional ways, and hold pro-business attitudes. They are not afraid to adopt technology if it is introduced in ways that accommodate their learning curve—but some have VCRs still flashing "12:00."

Primes may be "empty nesters" with adult children living on their own. Others are still raising children, as a result of delayed childrearing and second families born of second marriages. They tend to have their mortgages paid off and are generally better educated and more affluent than their parents were at the same age. These people will live longer than any previous generation, and are very conscious of their health, comfort, and self-fulfillment needs. They enjoy a broad spectrum of social activities and are interested in making the most of their precious spare time.

This "prime" segment—encompassing leading-edge baby boomers and pre-retirees—is critically important to credit unions. And credit unions need to begin to position themselves *now* to play a critically important role for primes. These members have financial needs to be addressed, and they know it. They are concerned with planning for their retirement. They need investment strategies designed for asset accumulation and capital growth. They may be responsible for the financial and physical well-being of elderly parents. Planning for decades of retirement can be daunting. Your credit union should be meeting the needs of these members with services and products designed specifically for them.

The "prime" segment—encompassing leading-edge baby boomers and pre-retirees—is critically important to credit unions.

Although they are savers, do not underestimate their potential for credit cards and personal loans. This segment contains the primary purchasers of luxury automobiles. Few, if any, will pay cash for a $30,000 car.

At this critical decision-making threshold, these members need to know that their credit union stands ready to assist them. If you do not communicate that the necessary products and services are available, these members are very likely to take their business elsewhere.

Within the next five years, the majority of primes will be baby boomers, who stand to inherit trillions of dollars from their own parents. It's likely primes will also assume greater stewardship of grandchildren. To forfeit these "redefiner boomers" as credit union members would amount to a staggering financial and moral loss for the movement.

Marketing Across the Generations: Some Overlaps

If you have read another book in this series, *Marketing Across the Generations: Baby Boomers (35–53),* you may already be familiar with our use of the verb "redefine" in connection with the massive baby boomer cohort. As those boomers move into middle adulthood, they bring their baby boomer perspective and energy with them, redefining what it means to be "mature." (Leading-edge boomers have been turning 50 at the rate of roughly 3 million per year since 1996.)

"Seniors" (late adults ages 65–79)

Active and independent, **seniors** are not yet old by many standards. The majority are members of the "silent generation," generally born between 1921 and 1942. Early life experiences for many were colored by the suffering of the Depression. Many left home for the army, rather than marriage. Still, they married young, and started families soon after. Whether blue-collar or white-collar, they sought jobs in large companies, fully expecting to rise through the ranks and stay for life. Silent men became the "lunch box Joes" and gray flannel suits who powered the engine of American economic expansion. Silent generation women became the "Betty Crocker" moms who pioneered the suburbs. For the most part, it is the silent generation we see depicted in early television dramas and sitcoms.

Most silents are socially dynamic retirees, interested in balancing their budgets and maintaining a high quality of life. They are security seekers, and they're patriotic and loyal.

This group provides an excellent market for financial planning services, which credit unions are well-positioned to address. Estate planning becomes important as they prepare to transfer wealth to children and grandchildren. Tax avoidance is an issue. Generally, silents/seniors tend to be more conservative and risk-averse in their investments. Convenience, quality service, and personal attention are high priorities.

Health care costs and long-term care services command greater attention in this group. Use of these services slowly increases, as does dependence on family and friends for help with chores, transportation, and recreation.

Elders (80-plus)

The majority of today's elders are members of the **G.I. generation.** Born between 1900 and 1920, this generation witnessed revolutions in technology, transportation, and information. Discipline and self-sacrifice were the building blocks of their characters. As they came of age, they were faced with rebuilding the world from the ground up—economically, politically, and socially. They took on the job, learning the value of teamwork and respect for authority as they went. Hard work and sacrifice paid off: they transformed America's standard of living.

Elders' early life experiences ran to Depression, war, and fear of foreign powers. Their attitudes toward life and work were molded by tough times. Their expectations were modest; their values, traditional. Hard work, obedience to authority, self-denial, and conservatism marked the points on this generation's moral compass.

When they were young, so was the financial services industry. People paid cash. Credit cards were unheard-of. Mortgage interest rates were low. Families saved for the holidays with dimes in coffee cans, not Christmas Clubs.

For most of their lives, members of the G.I. generation have gone without the extras. Even as they reached financial security, their style of spending reflected more cautious, disciplined values. Much of their saving and spending was for others, especially their children.

Today, two-thirds of people in this generation are women, and most are widowed. Access to affordable health care and maintaining a sufficient income are generally their highest priorities. Ill health and loss of independence are common, and many have difficulty with tasks that younger people take for granted. At this age individuals tend to concentrate more on daily self-care and a closer circle of family and friends.

Despite their increasing limitations, these members are vital to credit unions. In keeping with our social mission, credit unions become more vital to these members, who need assistance and advice with financial matters. We can help lighten the burden of coordinating the physical and financial close of their lives.

Figure 1.1 The Mature Market

Age Label	Middle Adults	Late Adults	Elders
Market segment	Primes	Seniors	Elders
Age in 2000	50–64	65–79	80–plus
Generational peers	Boomers/Silents	Silents	"G.I.s"

Figure 1.1 summarizes the naming structure we will use in discussing these major subgroups in relation to credit union marketing.

Managing Complexity. Ages, stages, new generational cohorts moving through them—are we recommending you have multiple market segmentation strategies going at all times, just to accommodate those of your members who happen to be over age 50? Well, actually, yes. To the extent your marketing resources allow you to manage such diversity, multiple target marketing strategies will pull better results than undifferentiated mass marketing strategies.

The purpose of this book is to encourage you to look beyond your stereotypes of your members over the age of 50. By doing so, you will develop a natural "feel" for the products, services, and messages appropriate to the major segments within the mature market. It's up to you to decide how to incorporate these insights into your marketing program. You may choose to pinpoint separate niches with individual marketing strategies, or rely on a broader program. A variety of examples are given in upcoming chapters.

RESEARCH: THE KEY TO TARGET MARKETING

Marketers use research to explore the current and evolving needs of potential target segments. Research techniques can be primary—gathered directly from first-hand sources—or secondary—gathered from existing sources such as research reports, census data, and case studies. Your Marketing Customer Information File (MCIF) provides an important means of primary research. The MCIF is a key tool available to credit unions to segment members by life stage and generational cohort. If you have an MCIF database, you already have access to the information that will help you develop your generational marketing strategy.

The MCIF is a key tool available to credit unions to segment members by life stage and generational cohort.

With the power of a database, you can segment your membership into smaller subgroups of members that are similar demographically, geographically, and financially. Use of an MCIF will lead to less expensive, more effective, and more profitable marketing campaigns and product packaging structures.

What makes MCIF programs so valuable is their ability to "marry" information in useful ways. The MCIF provides data preparation, query, analysis, and reporting tools. Consider the potential of querying with multiple search criteria. For example, you could use your MCIF to find members who:

- hold three or more accounts per household;
- use deposit products indicating affluence;
- fall within a certain age range; for example, are over age 65;
- have children within a certain age range, for example, over age 25; and
- do not have an employer.

This search is likely to result in a list of active, well-to-do, retired grandparents, who share silent generation character traits. These individuals are prime candidates for a credit union promotion focusing on intergenerational activities and opening special grandchildren's accounts.

Intergenerational Opportunities. The experience of Donna Zaccour, marketing director for Seaboard Credit Union in Jacksonville, Florida, indicates how well this can work. "Our youth club, the Dalmatian Club, offers activities and a special holiday Dalmatian certificate that requires a $500 initial deposit," she says. "We market that to seniors as a great gift to give. Those are real popular. Our seniors love to participate in the Dalmatian Club. They get their grandkids involved."

With a little creative thinking, a good MCIF database, and a list generated by the right multiple search criteria, all kinds of creative promotional campaigns are possible. A number of examples are presented throughout this book.

Other Forms of Research. Other forms of primary research can be important in building your mature marketing program. Consider conducting focus groups, scheduling individual information-gathering interviews with older members, and simply spending time where older people do. For secondary research, consult CUNA & Affiliates *Environmental Scan* and *Marketing by the Numbers* publications. Search out articles on mature marketing, and study relevant census data.

Full-scale market research is tough to do well, but critical to your success. We'll discuss market research techniques in greater detail in chapter 3. For the meantime, let's focus on the big picture:

- Market research is essential to a segmentation strategy.
- Segmentation strategies inspire enhanced products and services that better serve member needs.
- Serving member needs results in stronger member relationships.

And that's where we want to go.

THE MATURE MARKET IS VITAL

Most marketing sources will tell you it is eight to ten times easier to expand relationships with current members than to find and sign up new members. With ever-increasing competition from banks and other nonbank entities, credit unions must become the Primary Financial Institution (PFI) of choice for members if they are to maintain market share. Learning to use customer information to fine-tune market-

---

Snapshot
Be Sure Your Members Know: Once a Member, Always a Member

The mature market is vital to the long-term stability of credit unions. According to the U.S. Census Bureau, by 2020 this market will have grown 74 percent, while the population under age 50 will grow by only 1 percent. In spite of this, credit union membership continues to drop off at age 65. Recent research by CUNA & Affiliates indicates that many adult members of credit unions are unaware of their continuing eligibility for membership after age 65. Also surprising: many are unaware that their spouses and children are eligible members. Let them know: "Once a member, always a member."

---

ing efforts addresses that goal. This information can be used to strengthen existing relationships, and to facilitate cross-selling of additional services to those members.

The effort to serve members better generally leads credit unions to develop an enhanced product line. This same enhanced product line can be marketed to non-members. This progression—first focusing on retaining and strengthening existing member relationships, then using that momentum to attract new members—is both cost effective and manageable.

CREDIT UNION ACTION STEPS

- Review your credit union's previous and current segmentation strategies. Evaluate their success. What lessons can you learn from the past, as you prepare your future marketing plans?

- Picture individual members you are familiar with, who fit an age and a life stage segment described here. Consider how you could harvest insights from these individuals. Individual interviews? Focus groups? Surveys? Then give the same consideration to some familiar members who *don't* fit neat categories. Make a list of members who might participate in a research project.

- Most credit union marketers recognize the need to market to older members. But do your senior management and board understand the dynamic transformation of this market now underway? Consider preparing a presentation about segmentation strategies and the mature market, using this book as your guide.

OLDER MEMBERS' IMPORTANCE TO CREDIT UNIONS

"It's hard to understand why advertisers still can't bear to tear their sights away from consumers in their teens, twenties, and early thirties, at a time when spending power is becoming progressively more concentrated among those age 50 and older. Household income is highest for those age 45 to 54."

— *Richard A. Lee,* American Demographics

The mature consumer has been ignored by marketers for many years. Instead, marketers have tended to target products and services to younger generations. In part this is due to the age of marketers themselves: many are in their twenties and thirties. But even more practiced marketers tend to "worship" youthful attributes.

As (Not) Seen on TV. The majority of our perceptions about the world now come from movies and television. Informed by what we see there, we have difficulty imagining the vitality and variety of prime-life adults. Most prime-time television shows are still targeted to 18- to 35-year-olds, as are the products advertised during the commercial breaks. When matures are depicted, they still tend to be shown with stereotyped characteristics.

Recently, though, a refocusing is occurring, and the mature market is receiving quite a bit of attention. The weight of demographics is shifting the balance of spending power away from youth.

Mature Market Stealing the Show. As a result of longer life expectancies and the priming of baby boomers, the mature market has gained enormous economic strength. Today those age 50 and older make up more than 25 percent of the population— and that percentage is growing every day. By the year 2014, the 50-plus market will represent more than 34 percent of the U.S. population, at least 106 million consumers, according to the U.S. Census Bureau.

Families headed by someone over the age of 50 have income levels 35 percent above the U.S. mean.

The individuals behind those statistics are financially powerful. Families headed by someone over the age of 50 have income levels 35 percent above the U.S. mean. They control $800 billion in discretionary income. They have a combined annual household income of more than $1.5 trillion. While they make up only about a quarter of the population, matures:

- Control 77 percent of all financial assets
- Represent 66 percent of all stockholders in the United States
- Make up 80 percent of the luxury travel market

When pondering these statistics from the U.S. Census Bureau and *AgeWave* magazine, it's easy to see why this market has significance for financial institutions. They are fiscally active, stable, reliable, and conservative. They are profitable to serve, and loyal to those who provide good service. They demonstrate many of the characteristics we treasure in our best members.

What's more, mature members are influential within their family systems— often looked to for financial advice, including the choice of where younger relatives open their financial accounts. Prime-adult members are extremely influential in recruiting new, younger members to their own financial institutions. Much of their wealth is transferred to the next generation, a transition eased by housing family accounts under one (hopefully credit union) roof.

Retaining these strong members and building intergenerational financial relationships are vital strategies for your credit union.

WHERE HAVE THE MATURE MEMBERS GONE?

Credit union membership attrition above the age of 65, the traditional age of retirement, is significant. According to the CUNA & Affiliates 1998 National Member Survey, the 65-plus age group remains among the least served age groups. Market penetration of the senior and elder subsegments has increased only modestly during recent years. Three reasons readily come to mind:

1. Retired members are looking for convenient access to financial services—and convenience is no longer associated with a workplace.
2. Historically, credit unions have concentrated on making loans, primarily to younger members.
3. Competitors already have products and services in place and are actively soliciting our mature members' accounts.

Let's take a closer look.

Diminished Convenience

Convenience is the primary reason people join credit unions. One of the major conveniences is automatic payroll deductions for share account deposits and loan payments. Many members join credit unions at their places of employment—particularly at employer-sponsored credit unions, whose primary facilities are on-site at the companies. At retirement, many of these members end their financial relationships with the credit union. This is often due to a misperception—the belief that working for that employer is a requirement for membership. As marketers, we have not done enough to dispel myths about membership. (This aspect is explored further in chapter 7.)

Members who retire do, of course, cease coming to the job site and, in many cases, lose the convenience of on-site credit union facilities. This, too, is an issue we can address. Distribution of our services must be convenient to our members. And safe, reliable financial services delivered via computer make credit unions convenient even for home-bound members. Increasingly, matures are overcoming reluctance to use computers and access the Internet. (See snapshot titled, "Matures and Computers Are Matching Up.")

Focus on Lending

An unchallenged belief that lending is the core business of credit unions has kept the focus of many credit unions on younger members—who traditionally need to borrow for educations, cars, and homes. In past years, credit unions with high liquidity deliberately avoided promoting services to older members because they perceived them primarily as savers. With loan demand down and savings up, credit unions emphasized loans to younger members to increase loan-to-share ratios. As interest rates fell and their share certificates matured, these individuals flocked to brokerage firms and investment companies to take advantage of a bull market and to gain interest income.

More Competition

Many credit unions have neglected to encourage older members to stay with the credit union. And while we've been sleeping, other suitors have come calling.

Banks, in their envy of the affinity relationship that credit unions enjoy with members, are intent on developing new relationship-marketing techniques. Recognizing the mature market's value to the bottom line, they cater to individuals over age 50. Many have been successful in marketing to older customers by developing special programs to serve them.

In sum, credit unions have been less proactive than the competition in serving older members. Consequently, we have been largely unsuccessful in retaining these members.

SERVING MATURE MEMBERS

As the statistics quoted earlier reveal, the mature market controls tremendous financial assets. How can we help them manage those assets—to their great benefit as well as our own?

Especially today, when many credit unions are looking for deposits to fund loans, mature member accounts are one of the best sources of liquidity. Credit unions can benefit from developing a closer relationship with matures because they:

- Provide an immediate potential for deposits.
- Generally keep higher share and checking balances than younger members.
- Generally maintain more accounts per household than younger members.
- Use traditional credit union products, including auto loans and credit cards.
- Provide the largest potential market for cross-selling annuities, securities, and insurance.
- Still are borrowers at various life stages, especially baby-boomer primes.

It's time to re-examine our assumptions about the needs and desires of the 50-plus member.

Matures Are in the Market for Loans

Many credit union marketers accept the conventional wisdom that younger members are borrowers, older members are savers. This is overall a true perception. But there are many new niches within the mature market, and many of the individuals who occupy them are looking for loans.

Consider the following examples.

George is a successful executive nearing retirement. He's in the market for a loan to purchase a new luxury automobile. The cars he's looking at cost upward of $20,000. Is he going to pay cash? Even though he has the resources, he probably won't. Why pull investments out of a mutual fund that's earning 10 percent when he can take out a home equity line of credit, pay interest of approximately 8.5 percent, and earn a tax deduction. He may even consider a conventional auto loan more fiscally wise than parting with $20,000 cash that's invested at 10 percent. George is conservative fiscally, but uninterested in self-denial.

Carla just turned 70 and she's getting a new roommate—her 93-year-old aunt Elsa. She's eager to make this arrangement work, but the home in which she's lived for thirty years will need some adjustments to accommodate Elsa's needs. A remodeling loan will pay for a wheelchair ramp and a bathroom off the old den—Elsa's new bedroom. Carla is a silent-generation mom who continues to adapt for her family's welfare. In the course of bringing Elsa into her home, it's likely she will encourage "G.I. generation" Elsa to move her financial accounts to Carla's credit union.

Bud and Victoria aren't winding down—they're taking off. With the twins finally out of college, married and starting families of their own, this youthful, empty-nest couple is turning their attention to their own long-delayed dreams. They want to trade their big home for two small ones—a condo at home in the Midwest, and another in Florida near many of their friends. They're also looking to buy a recreational vehicle for trips between the two homes, and possibly some adventure travel out West as well. "We feel 30," says Bud. "Why shouldn't we live like it?" Bud and Victoria aren't afraid to borrow money to finance a lifestyle they've been looking forward to for years. Bud and Victoria are 53-year-old baby boomers ready to hit the road.

Martina, another boomer prime, retired from the utility company at age 55 to start her own web page design firm. She'd like to exchange some equity in her home for computer equipment and other business start-up costs. This is common. The number of older adults involved in "SOHO" businesses (Small Office/Home Office) is quite large, and likely to grow. Retired executives are starting consulting businesses. Empty-nester women and men are successfully turning hobbies into business opportunities. Consider exploring the business needs of your busy primes and seniors.

Empty-nester women and men are successfully turning hobbies into business opportunities.

As these snapshots show, there can be as many reasons to borrow as there are individuals with dreams. Credit unions can capitalize on the opportunity by helping older members fulfill their ambitions.

Mature Members Want Financial Advice—And More

Loans are the traditional strong suit of credit unions, but there's no reason for it to stay that way. Matures have multiple needs, and the credit union mission of "people helping people" should inspire us to help answer those needs.

Baby boomers, as a group, have the greatest need for financial planning. As they become the majority of primes during the next five years, their needs for sound retirement planning and provision for their aging parents will press with even greater urgency. Do you have the planning resources to assist them?

Help them plan for new life stages. Retirement can be a wonderful opportunity to fulfill lifelong dreams. Activities postponed for work or family can now be enjoyed. But only if there has been sound financial planning along the way.

To finance an active retirement, seniors need the best possible return on their investments. Many have underestimated their needs, and it's difficult for them to scale back their lifestyles. Returning to work may or may not be the answer.

How Can We Help? First and foremost, by providing financial education. Some matures are so overwhelmed by information on investing that many, including boomers, don't know where to turn. Anything you can do to simplify this information will be beneficial to them.

Financial education and planning is very important for women elders, especially those in the silent generation and G.I. generation cohorts. Many of these women left financial decisions to the men in their lives earlier on, and only recently have attempted to improve their financial literacy. Women outlive men by seven years, on average. Many earned lower wages and fewer benefits during their working years. Sound advice is needed, and you can help them find it.

Financial fraud is a real concern for your elder matures. Unscrupulous advisers and scam artists of all kinds are intent on exploiting them. Help your members protect themselves by giving them good information.

Credit unions have always taken pride in providing member education. Sponsoring retirement planning seminars will provide your prime-age members with a valuable educational opportunity. Using your own staff and local resources, you can provide an educational forum that encourages members to think through and plan for the many changes their bonus years will bring them.

In addition to helping your members plan their financial strategies, your credit union can also help them prepare for the nonfinancial aspects of retirement. Credit unions offer seminars on these topics and more:

- Health and fitness
- Time management
- Travel opportunities
- Wellness and nutrition
- Housing needs and options
- Volunteer opportunities
- Legal affairs and estate planning

Seminars give members a chance to socialize, share ideas, and renew their bonds of loyalty to the credit union and its members. Such activities show members that the credit union is more than a financial institution. Reinforce the bond that serves you both.

Mature Members Believe in Credit Unions

Many of your senior and elder members have been the backbone of the credit union movement throughout their lives. When for-profit banks were failing, communities got together and formed nonprofit financial institutions—credit unions—to serve their needs. Young families turned to us to help them through hard times during the Great Depression. Our payroll-deduction savings plans helped with their children's education. Our loans helped veterans buy homes after the war. Now it's time for both credit unions and older members to enjoy the rewards of our shared history.

Those members who needed us for loan products then are now starting to need us for other services—including some that a nonprofit charter precludes. We can let those needs be met by banks, investment firms, and insurance brokers, but in doing so we take a pass on the opportunity to serve as their primary financial institution (PFI). In order to meet more member needs, and build stronger PFI relationships, many credit unions start or join credit union service organizations (CUSOs).

Primary Financial Institutions: PFIs

Individuals have many options for meeting their financial service needs. Most individuals, for convenience if nothing else, consolidate the majority of their financial relationships under one roof. This institution is known as their primary financial institution, or PFI. Historically, credit unions have been slow to pursue PFI status with their members, but our marketers are working to close that gap.

What Are CUSOs? Credit Union Service Organizations (CUSOs) are alternative, for-profit vehicles established by credit unions to market such products as annuities, insurance, and mutual funds. Credit unions establish CUSOs because regulations prohibit us from marketing alternative financial products: In addition to mutual funds, annuities, and life insurance, a CUSO can offer health insurance, disability and long-term care, as well as investment advice, estate planning, and stock brokerage.

The credit union's marketing efforts—especially cross-selling by member service representatives—should encourage members to extend their trust in the credit union to its CUSO subsidiary. The CUSO benefits from identification with the credit union—and the members benefit from access to the broader range of products and services offered by the CUSO. It's not unusual for up to 80 percent of a CUSO's business to come from existing members of its parent credit union. People coming into their credit union are already thinking about money—it's not hard to convince them to consider the CUSO's offerings. CUSOs will be discussed further in the next chapter, as we turn our attention to developing product offerings for matures.

Mature Women and Credit Unions: A Good Match

There is a hidden opportunity that begins to come to light when we examine the demographic makeup of the mature market. The majority of matures are women. Women make good members of credit unions—and credit unions make good financial institutions for women. This observation is not limited to women of mature years, of course—but since we're studying the generational cohorts that make up the 50-plus age group, let's spend a moment looking at the match between mature women and credit unions.

Where mature women are concerned, the differences between each generational cohort are thrown into high relief. Women of the G.I. generation may have gone to work alongside "Rosie the Riveter" during World War II, but for the most part they laid down their lunch boxes willingly when the war was over. Building a family was the work they chose, when given a choice.

Silent generation women came of age amid that postwar domesticity. Some questioned the limitations of women's roles—as evidenced by Betty Friedan's ground-breaking book, *The Feminine Mystique*, first published in 1963. By the time Gloria Steinem (a true-to-type prime) began publishing *Ms.* magazine in 1972, a social shift of dramatic proportions had taken place. By 1980, over 50 percent of women were participating in the American workforce, according to *Rocking the Ages.*

Silent generation women came of age amid postwar domesticity.

According to psychographic research, women are highly affiliative and loyal to relationships. Credit unions aspire to be highly affiliative and to win relationship loyalty—there should be a powerful and mutually dynamic fit. But few credit unions have, in the past, made any special effort to develop relationships with women. Our survey of current research reveals we would be wise to begin pursuing these relationships, especially where mature women are concerned. They like us, and we like them.

The evolution of women's roles vis-a-vis financial matters highlights the importance of generational cohorts. Women over age 65 tend to be much less savvy regarding their finances than their younger "sisters" are. Marketers should selectively address their messages to women primes, or to women who are seniors and elders. Attempting to reach both with a common message is likely to miss the mark, given their very different beliefs and backgrounds. (We'll explore marketing messages and generational cohorts further in chapter 7.)

More Matures are Women (But Are Women More Mature?)

Fifty-eight percent of Americans over age 65 are women, compared to only 42 percent who are men. (There are no "undecideds.") Life expectancy for women is 79.67 years, compared to 72.95 years for men. The older the slice of America you look at, the more women you see. Source: U.S. Census Bureau Data, July 1999.

Bringing Back the Good Old Days (and Good Old Members)

It's time to turn around the tendency to allow attrition of older members for whatever combination of reasons. New strategies, based on understanding older members' needs, are in order. Let's rework our products, services, and marketing messages to reflect our desire to fill members' needs at every life stage.

Where to begin? With a strategic marketing process, resulting in a specific, actionable marketing plan. This book explores that process in depth in the next two chapters.

The 50-plus market will be the dominant demographic force in America for at least the next thirty years. The 76-million-member baby boom generation is turning 50 at the rate of 300,000 a month. They are changing the marketing landscape just as they changed every demographic vista before. By the year 2030, the total number of retirement-age people will hit 65 million. With continued economic prosperity, longer life spans, and improved health care, we are talking about affluent, healthy, well-educated, and vibrant individuals. Capitalize on the enormous potential represented by this demographic group. Help them experience the credit union difference.

CREDIT UNION ACTION STEPS

- Generate a list of closed accounts. Can you identify why these members have lapsed? Was it in search of convenience and/or better savings vehicles, or because a competitor wooed them away? Do you know what institutions these ex-members consider their PFI? Write a few notes summarizing your observations. Group these lapsed members by generational cohort and life stage attributes. Do any patterns appear?

- Take a seat in the lobby for one hour in the middle of the morning or afternoon. (Let the member services representatives know what you are doing.) Record your observations of older members. What services do they use? What would their MCIF records tell you about them, and others like them? What can the tellers and other member contact people add to your understanding of them?

- Look at your deposit accounts by age: group them as primes, seniors, and elders. What does this show you about the importance of older members?

FOCUSING THE STRATEGIC MARKETING PROCESS ON THE MATURE SEGMENT

"If you fail to plan, you plan to fail."

— *Rory Rowland*, Credit Union Magazine

Is planning your favorite part of the marketing process? Probably not. Still, if you intend to be successful in your generational marketing effort, a good plan will be required.

According to recent CUNA research, about 50 percent of U.S. credit unions have a written marketing plan. How is the half that have written plans different from the half that does not? The credit unions with plans tend to be characterized by larger assets (more than $50 million), or by common bonds that include multiple groups. Both of these characteristics would suggest that target marketing strategies are being used. Why?

Planning for Target Marketing. Credit unions with larger assets typically also have larger, more diverse member bases, with a broad range of demographic, geographic, and lifestyle traits. Likewise, credit unions whose common bond includes several unique groups are also likely to have members demonstrating diverse characteristics.

Credit unions of either type tend to study their members, looking for subgroups with collections of traits that predict the needs and desires of unique segments. The result is a target marketing strategy. Coordinating different marketing goals tailored to different target markets is made easier by a written marketing plan. That's the story behind the statistic.

Your credit union does not have to match the description of the 50 percent with plans to benefit from your own written plan. If that 50 percent were to become 100 percent, the credit union movement would be that much stronger. We suggest you develop a written marketing plan to guide your generational marketing program.

THE STRATEGIC MARKETING PROCESS

Five Steps to Strategic Marketing

The strategic marketing process, as summarized in CUNA & Affiliates' *Credit Union Marketing Handbook,* follows these steps:

1. Determine the organization's missions and objectives.
2. Assess the organization's opportunities, threats, and resources.
3. Choose core marketing strategies.
4. Prepare a detailed marketing plan to carry out the core strategies.
5. Measure and evaluate performance.

Mission and Objectives. How does one "determine an organization's missions and objectives"? It would be flippant to say "You ask your boss" but, in fact, that's not far off. Your credit union most likely has developed an overall strategic plan. This plan addresses organizational vision, mission, and objectives. One reason such a long-term plan has been developed is to help guide you, and other strategic business units such as lending and human resources, in developing your own strategic plans. The plan for each business unit is based on the overall strategic plan. Your marketing plan, then, is based on your unit's strategic plan, which is based on the overall organizational strategic plan. Begin by reviewing existing strategic planning documents, and interviewing senior management regarding their long-range visions for your credit union.

Assessment. As part of that planning process, your senior management probably conducted a situational analysis, examining your relative strengths and weaknesses, threats, and resources. Revisit that analysis now. You may find that it was performed some time ago, and needs to be freshened with current insights. You may also find that from your perspective as a marketer, you see elements in the competitive environment, your membership base, or your organization, that hold special relevance for marketing planning, but that were not addressed by the strategic plan.

To arrive at a marketing plan, you must look both inward and outward. What's your organization bringing to the party, and what's going on when you get there? Internal interviews will help you understand what you can bring to the party, in terms of product mix, distribution methods, pricing, and promotional messages. External information-gathering will fuel the process of matching what you offer to what your marketplace is looking for.

To arrive at a marketing plan, you must look both inward and outward.

Your external information-gathering should include both qualitative and quantitative market research, focused on understanding your members, your prospective members, and your competitors.

Choosing Strategies. Having studied both internal and external factors, you must now choose the core marketing strategies that will move you forward toward organizational objectives. As you can imagine, it doesn't happen overnight, and it doesn't happen alone. Your organization's top management must be involved, and adequate background information must be available to them. Such weighty decision-making requires sufficient inputs. Summarize the findings of your situational assessment. Present statistical information generated from your Marketing Customer Information File (MCIF) or other sources. Write a marketing brief summarizing your insights and observations so far. A brainstorming session with top management is recommended at this stage.

Let's assume your situational assessment suggests that generational marketing will be effective for you. A core marketing strategy will be to pursue target market segments defined by age, generational cohort, and life stage. With such a strategy, you can pinpoint homogenous niches within the mature market for precisely tailored product and/or service offerings.

Once a target market has been selected, you face a number of decisions. What sorts of products and services should be offered to them? How should these be priced? How promoted? How delivered? Your answers to these questions become your core strategies. A target marketing program designed to address niches within the mature market will include a specific core strategy designed to appeal to specific needs and wants.

Preparing a Plan. Your detailed marketing plan can only take shape once core strategies have been chosen. The marketing plan will address advertising concerns, such as message themes, media plan, and budget. It will also address operational issues, such as training of staff to communicate the program, and changes required in your retail environment, distribution channels, and so on. This marketing plan includes all the details necessary for implementation of the core strategies.

Evaluation. Your process will not be complete until you have measured and evaluated your plan's performance. To do that, you must set realistic goals, and define a means for evaluating whether those goals have been met. A benchmark is a point of reference by which future performance will be judged. It tells you whether your results are better than expected, worse than expected, or right on target.

Your benchmark might be the number of new accounts opened, or number of members enrolled in your 60-plus club, or number of attendees at a seminar. Each marketing initiative should be accompanied by a performance benchmark.

Document your results, and compare them to benchmarks. This may be challenging at first, when you have little data on which to base your predictions. You will find it becomes easier with experience and the passage of time.

What Do You Know? The Importance of Research

The most essential work of market planning lies in matching a product offering to needs and wants of a market segment—and doing so in a way that competitors have not. Information about member needs, competitors' strategies, and your own ability to create a desirable product offering are required.

Where your mature market member segment is concerned, you may not have conducted much research in the past. Typically, credit union marketers have focused on promoting loans, and so we have devoted our research efforts to understanding the younger segments of our membership—those members who are statistically more likely to borrow. This may leave us in the dark when it comes to understanding our older members' needs.

What Do You Know About Your Mature Members?

Research is a way to explore the evolving needs of the older member as a target segment. Credit unions can take advantage of a variety of research techniques to understand our mature members. The following examples illustrate how several credit unions have made use of research to learn about their matures.

> *Credit unions can take advantage of a variety of research techniques to understand our mature members.*

Vista Federal Credit Union in Burbank, California, uses an MCIF augmented with census bureau data, to perform segmentation by life stage analysis. "We can look at the full relationship members have with us," reports Jeff York, vice president of marketing. "We can find members who are 55-plus, have only $5,000 in combined deposits with us, yet make $125,000 a year. We know that's a good group to go to, to attract deposits. Especially when our rates will beat anybody else around."

Vista FCU has performed annual surveys of its membership since 1992. Its survey instrument includes age demographics, resulting in an evolving understanding of the membership population. "We learn what products and services they want," York continues. "Eight years ago we were almost plain vanilla. Now we're a full-service worldwide credit union. We've changed quite a bit in those eight years." York feels the annual survey has helped fuel the credit union's growth.

Meanwhile, CUNA Credit Union in Madison, Wisconsin, has used its MCIF to create a random sample for a telephone survey. In addition, says Marketing Director Amy Crowe: "We have PRIZM codes attached to our MCIF. The codes tell us what products members buy, what they do with their time. This helps us target courtesy calls, to invite older members to special events that will interest them."

Seaboard Credit Union in Jacksonville, Florida, uses member surveys both to gather information and to give information. Marketing Director Donna Zaccour describes her approach: "We have an outside company do a telephone survey, and we have in-house written surveys, and we always have a suggestion box in the lobby. We listen to members.

"On the surveys are service questions—how we can improve, what we could offer—and then there are product questions—rate comparisons, time frames for certificates, and so on. The telephone survey of members is quite lengthy. It's a random survey, but we do make sure we include a lot of seniors in the list, because we want to make sure we're taking care of them. We do the survey in a way that is informative, but it's a marketing tool, too. We'll describe a product, and ask if you might want to try it."

Mature Members Wary of Phone "Survey" Scams

Amy Crowe of CUNA Credit Union has this advice concerning phone surveys: "Older members like the personal touch, but they're wary of scams. When we call them we're careful how we introduce ourselves. We'll say something like 'I'm Carla, from CUNA Credit Union, calling about our V.I.P. Club.' We don't want to confuse them. We let them know right up front it's just a courtesy call."

Research Techniques. Techniques for market research include those described in the above examples—querying your internal customer database, and member surveys—but there are many more options available. Research can be qualitative or quantitative, and it can be gathered either from direct or indirect sources. Qualitative research is anecdotal, open-ended, and feelings-based. Quantitative research, on the other hand, draws on statistical analysis of measurable data. Querying your database would be classified as quantitative, direct research. Purchasing data from an outside vendor would be quantitative but indirect—not gathered directly by you. If you invited older members to participate in a focus group, that would be qualitative direct research. If you read an article about one credit union's generational marketing program in *Credit Union Journal,* that would be qualitative indirect research.

Indirect sources of data include:

- Government sources, for example, the U.S. Census Bureau
- Industry sources, such as CUNA & Affiliates and NCUA

- Media sources—research performed by trade journals, the financial press, and others
- Private sources, such as commercial databases

Direct sources of information include your members, potential members, and subject matter experts who may be found on the faculties of local educational institutions, in the private sector, and even on your own board. Direct research can be conducted via focus groups, interviews, observation, and surveys. The list doesn't stop there—but to continue is beyond the scope of our discussion. For more information about market research, consult your state league. You may be referred to resource people or useful books, such as CUNA CPD's *Market Research Made Easy* or other CUNA publications.

Members Share Certain Expectations. No matter what type of research you conduct, and how in-depth you pursue the research project, you are likely to arrive at certain conclusions regarding the expectations of your members and potential members.

One thing all individuals share, regardless of their generational or other segmentation characteristics, is a desire to be well-informed. Your members want options, and they want to know the pros and cons of each option. What are the benefits to them, both short- and long-term? Your members want truths—not marketing hype or hard-sell pitches. People want to do business with trusted professionals offering sound solutions to real problems.

People want to do business with trusted professionals offering sound solutions to real problems.

People also share a desire to be treated ethically. Guileless consumers can be pressured into making decisions they don't understand. No one wants to be sold a product they don't really need. CUNA's Marketing Council developed a code of ethical behavior for credit union marketers (reprinted here in figure 3.1). The code supports the professional and personal standards of conduct befitting an employee of a member-owned nonprofit financial institution. Our social responsibility and professional ethics are cornerstones of our movement. That makes us attractive to potential members—and it's a trust we must not damage.

Figure 3.1 CUNA Marketing Council's Standards of Conduct

As credit union marketing professionals and members of the CUNA Marketing Council (CMC), we dedicate ourselves to the highest ethical standards of professional and personal conduct.

In the matter of honesty . . . We will be party only to marketing, advertising, or public relations that reflect the truth of our institutions as we understand it. Our goal is to use absolute honesty to deepen the credibility of our marketing efforts and by extension, our credit unions, and the credit union movement.

In the matter of integrity . . . We recognize and appreciate credit unions as financial cooperatives that share both ideas and opportunities among its professional practitioners. At no time will we abuse that privilege and assume ownership of marketing ideas, approaches, or techniques developed by other marketing professionals without prior permission.

In the matter of community . . . We understand the value of credit unions to their communities, both geographic and demographic, and will commit our allocable resources to support our communities. This includes serving internal and external customers selflessly, as well as avoiding social and political situations and alliances that would hamper our ability to serve.

In the matter of confidentiality . . . We support the importance of both institutional and individual confidentiality in the financial services industry. We pledge to uphold all confidentialities entrusted to us as both personal and professional obligations.

In the matter of gratuity . . . We realize that, regardless of fact, improper or excessively expensive gifts or rewards may indicate that decisions or favors can be bought. In the interest of the highest levels of integrity, such gifts or perquisites must not be accepted. This may also include the acceptance of honorariums for presentations made on behalf of the industry or individual institutions.

In the matter of accountability . . . We accept the value and importance of maintaining high personal and professional ethical standards, and we pledge our accountability to all previously mentioned guidelines and standards. This includes honesty in dealing with members, community, and the media; and integrity in representing the credit union and the members it serves.

Source: CUNA Marketing Council, "Standards of Conduct" (Credit Union National Association, Madison, WI, 1993). Reprinted with permission.

Generational Insights into Satisfaction. Individuals of different ages and life stages tend to have different perceptions of their financial needs, but most people share a desire for wise counsel. Many matures have gone years without seeking financial advice. Now they're facing complex financial choices. They don't want to make them alone. With so much at stake, wrong choices or delayed choices may lead to irretrievably lost opportunities. Most individuals look to their financial institution for leadership in this unfamiliar territory. As credit unions, we serve these members best when we are proactive in helping them plan for financial health. Our expertise translates to the leadership these individuals seek. This is especially important to mature members.

Do you know anyone who prefers shabby treatment to "first class"? Still, each individual has his or her own definition of "first class." As marketers, we strive to tailor our treatment of customers to each individual's perception of "first-class treatment." This is one reason generational segmenting succeeds. You get the best results from your interactions and messages when you communicate in the way people prefer to receive their information. Mature members prefer more formality and courtesy in interactions; they prefer detailed, well-written information when they read. Younger members might reject as "stuffy and uncool" messages that might evoke feelings of comfort and familiarity for older members.

> *Younger members might reject as "stuffy and uncool" messages that might evoke feelings of comfort and familiarity for older members.*

And finally, people prefer simplicity over complexity. We want products and services that simplify our lives. Simplicity comes in many forms—some may be attracted to the high-tech convenience of time-savers like PC-based financial services. Others' idea of simplicity might be automated telephone financial services. The point is, as marketers, we must find ways to make our offerings *seem* simple. Mature members may respond better to friendly personal support, or large print reference guides, than to services designed to simplify life via technological avenues.

These shared expectations are summarized in figure 3.2.

Figure 3.2 Expectations All Consumers Share

- Good information
- Ethical conduct
- **Leadership**
- **First-class treatment**
- **Simplicity**

Generally, expectations shown in bold are more deeply valued by mature consumers.

Nonmembers: Just Members You Haven't Met? What you know about members tells you a great deal about potential members. Most credit union marketers tend to focus on relationships with current members. It's relatively easy to sell new services to current members, compared to finding and converting nonmembers to members. However, if you focus solely on cross-selling, you will eventually limit your credit union's growth. There are realistic limits to how many of your services members will use. For long-term growth, you must also focus a portion of your attention on nonmembers. Using the demographic characteristics of your current members, you can identify nonmembers who resemble your best members, and who are likely to share similar needs, desires, and reactions to marketing messages. While this may require purchasing a mailing list, or devoting some of your marketing budget to mass media advertising, these investments will return a dividend of long-term growth.

What Do You Know About Your Competitors?

While you are busy learning about your members and potential members, so is someone else. At least one someone, and possibly more. In today's financial services marketplace, the competition never sleeps. You need to know what the competition is doing. Competitors can kill your best-laid plans, even if those plans are flawless in their logic, breathtaking in their accuracy and insight.

Who are your competitors? One or two names probably come to mind even as you read that sentence. One might be the big bank with the advertising budget that dominates the local airwaves. Another might be the credit union down the street, where they've done an exceptional job with their own marketing. But when you view the big picture, you see that many competitors exist in the marketplace. These include mortgage and finance companies, nonbank credit card issuers, and financial planners, just to name a few. With the rise of Internet financial service offerings, geography is no longer limiting the field of competitors. You are or soon will be, quite literally, in competition with every financial service provider with an Internet presence in the entire country and beyond.

Reviewing your competitors can often bring to light new opportunities for market segmentation. In studying your competition, you gain several important advantages:

- You may see an opening to win share of market from your competition, by recruiting their customers to your institution.
- Knowing their marketing strategies, including marketing mix and segmentation strategies, improves your ability to make your own marketing strategies unique, not "me-too."
- By observing your competition over time, you have the opportunity to learn from their mistakes.

Keep Tabs on Competitors. Quite naturally, your competitors are not going to reveal their marketing strategies to you before they are implemented. Your access to information about competitors' market share, budgets, segmentation strategies, and product development will be limited. However, you must search out the clues available to you. Pay close attention to newspaper reports. Keep tabs on the promotional efforts of competitors. Track product offerings, such as rates. Don't be afraid to send a "mystery shopper" to visit competitors. An older employee who visits that big bank and inquires about seniors' clubs will bring back a bonanza of information.

Here are a few other ideas for gaining competitive intelligence:

- Speak to suppliers, such as temporary staffing agencies, who do business with both you and your competition. You won't, of course, ask for trade secrets—but a casual, "Say, are they hiring over there at Big Bank?" will gain you useful clues.
- Other members of the business community, such as real estate developers, are likely to be in the know. General trends, and even quite specific information, are easy to obtain if you stay in touch with your peers in the community.

- Employees of your credit union often hold pieces of the puzzle, although they don't realize it. Staff members may have information from their peers in similar jobs with competitors. Your member service representatives or call center staff are likely hearing what the other guy is offering. Make time to gather that information.

What Was the Question? What is it you most want to know about your competitors? Remember, your goal is to create a unique and appealing mature segment marketing plan. You need to know how your competitors are addressing the 50-plus market. Ask yourself these questions about each competitor: What products are they pitching to the mature market? At what prices? How are they distributing the product or service? How are they promoting it? What share of the total market do they control? What are the strengths and weaknesses of their approach? The answers to these questions will influence the program you develop.

What Are the Components of Your Mature Market Program?

What products and services are your mature members likely to want from you? Your answer should include a combination of tangibles and intangibles. Your members may be looking for products in the infancy of the product life cycle, like long-term-care insurance, or in decline, like paper checking accounts (soon to be replaced by debit cards). Many credit unions are establishing Credit Union Service Organizations (CUSOs) to enable them to offer expanded product lines to older members, including investment and insurance services.

Your mature market program will need to include a pricing strategy. Typically, mature market programs offer free or discounted services to members who qualify for the program. For the seniors and elders in your membership, a cost savings appeal is effective, since these people tend to be frugal. But for your primes, price is often not so important. For those embarking on an affluent retirement, convenient access to services is more important than a few pennies saved.

Typically, mature market programs offer free or discounted services to members who qualify for the program.

You needn't build more branches to offer more convenience, however. Credit unions have augmented their convenience to members by establishing telephone call centers and Internet-based home financial services.

If you're going to develop a mature market program, it follows that you're going to want to promote it. Your advertising messages, when and where you advertise, the sales promotions you engage in—all must be components of your marketing plan. We'll discuss promotion in greater depth in upcoming chapters.

MATURES BELONG IN YOUR LONG-RANGE PLANS

What are the long-range goals of your credit union? Does the mature market fit well those long-term plans? Some credit unions, by nature of their fields of membership, tend to draw most of their members from younger age groups. Vista Federal Credit Union, introduced earlier in this chapter, is one.

Vista FCU is the employee credit union for the Walt Disney Company. Not surprisingly, attractions like Disneyland and Disney World employ a large number of young people. As a result, Vista has about 53,000 members with an average member age of 37—five years younger than the national credit union average member age of 42. Length of membership at Vista FCU averages only six to eight years—about half the national average of twelve to fifteen years of membership.

Jeff York of Vista explains why a credit union with such a young member base is interested in marketing to older adults.

"We want to cement our relationship with our older membership. We feel we need to focus on that group because, when the transfer of wealth happens from the baby boomers' parents to the baby boomers, the estimates are now upwards of $30 trillion changing hands. If we're doing a good job serving older members now,

---

The Goal: One-to-One Relationships with Members

Credit unions don't look for customers: we look for member relationships. Once we form a relationship with a member, we want it to last a lifetime. The way we approach that goal is to strive to customize our services, products, and messages to fit each member's needs, to the extent such one-to-one customization is possible. By approaching our mature members as individuals who fit niches within that larger population, we come closer to that one-to-one relationship. Our study of generational cohorts and life stages helps us understand these niches, in order to serve *individual members* better.

---

once that money transfers, we won't have that money going out the door. One reason we started [our CUSO] Castle Financial Services was that it's a great way to satisfy the needs of those members who will be inheriting wealth, or are moving into retirement years. Starting Castle Financial Services gave us the vehicle to go out and help people with financial planning, with retirement planning. Nine out of ten people who retire at age 65 go back to work within a year. We don't want our older members to have to go back . . . and start over, because they didn't plan properly for retirement."

As Vista FCU's example shows, you don't have to have an established older membership base to benefit from a mature market strategy. In the next chapter, we'll lay out the tactics that support a solid mature marketing plan and look at several credit unions' marketing programs.

CREDIT UNION ACTION STEPS

- Locate any strategic planning documents that exist, and make contact with the people who wrote them, if possible. Explain that you are considering a mature marketing strategy and are working on your plan.

- Review the market research resources that may be available to you. Consult with the person responsible for your MCIF or other database. Seek out any other research work that may have been done in the past: surveys, focus-group results, member suggestions.

- Consider what information about your competitors is most critical to you as you develop your marketing strategies. Who are your top three competitors? What do you know about their mature market offerings? Do they address primes differently than seniors? Seniors differently than elders?

Creating a Tactical Marketing Plan for the Mature Segment

"Branding is a way for a credit union to differentiate itself and build relationships with members on more than products and services. The challenge of branding is to position your credit union more strongly with consumers and members in terms of awareness, relevance, quality, and most important, competitive differentiation."

— *Pam Varela*, Marketing By the Numbers

It's 9:00 a.m. on a Tuesday. In Wisconsin, a group of retired CUNA employees gather to carpool to a nearby marsh for a nature walk. Across the Mississippi in Iowa, another group of older credit union members embark for a riverboat cruise. In Florida, a small group of elders gathers in a credit union meeting room to plan their annual benefit event. In California, 50- to 60-year-old employees of the gas company listen to a presentation on investment planning, a new service only recently available to them through their credit union.

What's going on here? Tactical marketing. Each activity—club outings, charitable work, informational seminars—is part of a credit union's marketing plan for matures. Let's look closer at two of the tactical marketing plans developed by these credit unions.

Dupaco Community Credit Union's Prime Time Club

Snapshot
Dupaco Community Credit Union

Dubuque, Iowa
Members: 34,000
Assets: $225 million
Field of Membership: Originally formed for the employees of the Dubuque Packing Company. Expanded to a community charter in 1996, covering five counties in eastern Iowa. Expanded again to seventeen counties in 1999.

"With our Prime Time Club we attempt to reward member loyalty, and build and enhance members' relations with the credit union," says Joe Hearn, senior vice president of marketing. The Dupaco Prime Time Club is open to members age 50 or older, with combined balances of over $1,500 in either deposits or loans. About 5,000 households are enrolled in the club. Those households control a very large percentage of Dupaco's total deposits. But that's only part of the reason we've made a strategic objective of enhancing those members' bond with the credit union."

Dupaco's Prime Time Club places an emphasis on events and activities. "We provide interactive social events, where we bring people to the credit union, or we organize events outside the credit union. We want the club to be of value to the members, so we organize these events and activities around their interests. We encourage them to bring guests," Hearn explains. Dupaco has found that Prime Time Club members are proud of their credit union and their club. They appreciate that their credit union takes time to organize events and activities of interest to them.

The Club Coordinator Is Important. Joe Hearn credits the success of Dupaco's Prime Time Club activities to the efforts of the club coordinator and other active participants. "We recruit active senior members to help host the events, coordinate them, collect the money and so on, so they take ownership in their club. That's worked out well for us," says Hearn. A dynamic part-time employee, herself returned from retirement, serves as club coordinator. "She organizes the events, and we support her. The marketing department puts out the newsletter, and the phone center takes the reservations and answers questions. Then she executes the events," he continues. Club activities vary from card parties to day trips, and even extended tours overseas.

Other Dupaco Prime Time Club benefits include:

- An identification card that garners discounts with local business partners, as well as enhanced rates on share certificates.
- Quarterly *Prime Time News* newsletter (described in chapter 7, shown in figure 7.1).
- Financial education via newsletter articles and seminars.
- Investment services through Dupaco Financial Services (a CUSO) and Financial Network Investment Corporation.

Where are the waived ATM fees, discounted check printing, and other typical components of a "Seniors' Club"? Dupaco has chosen not to bundle discounts on the credit union's own products and services with club membership. "We provide good value for all members. We don't really need to bonus the seniors a lot. The focus of the club is more on the social activities we offer," says Hearn.

Quite a few members of the Prime Time Club have been credit union members their whole lives. Not all, however. The club's focus on dynamic activities has resulted not just in retention of older members, but recruitment of new older members as well. "Our Prime Time members are our best recruiters. They believe in the credit union. They like what we're doing, they have fun, and they want their friends to join them."

An analysis of the Dupaco Prime Time Club reveals the marketing tactics behind the club's success.

Description of the Program. Features of the Prime Time Club include a wide range of activities of interest to its mostly senior members. Most activities are open to their guests as well. The club is designed to reward members' loyalty, and to enhance their relationship with their credit union. The club, started in 1988, has slowly built to its current dynamic status. It's stable and likely to grow due to overall population trends and future deposit marketing plans.

Dupaco has chosen not to include discount pricing, reflecting the good value of the credit union's rates for all members, when compared to local competitors.

Members participate in club activities, which take place in a variety of locations. Dupaco provides logistical support via the phone center's handling of activity reservations, busing arrangements, and such.

How It's Promoted. *Prime Times News* is the main vehicle for promoting the club's activities, as well as delivering club benefits such as financial education and member news. One of the most popular features of the newsletter is a column titled, "Prime Time Profile," which features a club members' interests, activities, and background with the credit union. Dupaco is aggressive in promoting its general products and services, and in community involvement. The result has been top-of-mind awareness among credit unions in a local survey conducted by the newspaper. There is some carryover effect from this public perception of Dupaco, which helps promote the Prime Time Club.

The Dupaco Objective. The Prime Time Club is designed to reward member loyalty, while building and enhancing member relations with the credit union. Results have been excellent, and no major changes are envisioned in the near future.

CUNA Credit Union's V.I.P. Club

Snapshot
CUNA Credit Union

Madison, Wisconsin
Members: 42,000
Assets: $172 million
Field of membership: Anyone in southern Wisconsin.

"At CUNA Credit Union we're savvy, progressive, ahead of the game. The goal of our club is to enhance the lives of our older members, with products and services tailored to their needs," says Amy Crowe, Marketing Supervisor. "Our mission is to find the *next* service members will need."

The CUNA Credit Union V.I.P. Club is open to members 60 years of age or older—a requirement changed in the mid-nineties from age 50, to limit membership to those with more similar needs and interests. By doing so, CUNA Credit Union displayed an instinctive understanding of the importance of pinpointing niches within the large and diverse mature market.

With the start of 1999, this credit union launched an initiative to rejuvenate the club. This effort included informal surveying of members to find out what they would like their club to offer, as well as a redesign of the newsletter to more closely reflect the dynamic lifestyles and interests of its members. "We renamed it *Cruising Power,* because our members are so active," Crowe explains. "Everybody we talk to is always on the go."

CUNA Credit Union's club requires a balance of $5,000 in a savings vehicle. Currently the club has about 1,500 members enrolled. The club includes both activities and an attractive bundle of products and services. Club activities include a walking club, visits to local points of interest, educational seminars, and annual picnics and holiday parties.

Other V.I.P. Club benefits include:

- A V.I.P. checking account with waived checking fees. The V.I.P. account earns dividends on an average daily balance of $750 or more.
- Waived limits on withdrawals from Wisconsin ATM machines.
- Free debit card (waived $6 fee).
- Quarterly *Cruising Power* newsletter.
- Free custom checks.
- Free money orders.
- Free photocopies.
- Free first year's membership in MEMBERS Prime Club, an affiliate of CUNA & Affiliates and CUNA Mutual Group.

Crowe describes the V.I.P. Club's activities:

"The club has outings once a month. Different segments go on different trips. The biggest challenge with the club is planning the events. Our members are so busy. If an event is on a Tuesday, that conflicts with somebody's golf game. And if it's on Thursday, that conflicts with the day they volunteer at the hospital. So we try to vary the times, places, and activities. We always plan several pickup points, so we're convenient for everybody.

"This year I've been talking with individuals, going to the events, asking questions like 'What do you do in your spare time? How far out of town would you like to go? How much would you pay? Would you rather we organized a bus, or carpools?' I get great ideas from the members."

Many V.I.P. Club members have been credit union members most of their lives. "They're loyal to the hilt," Crowe says. "At every event members come up and tell me stories about the old days. They feel loyalty to the credit union cause. But," she adds, "that doesn't mean we have all their money. Many have accounts all over town."

That represents an opportunity for enhanced relationships. Crowe encourages these via newsletter articles and financial planning seminars. CUNA Credit Union invites MEMBERS Financial Services representatives to help V.I.P. members recognize more ways their credit union can serve their financial needs.

An analysis of the V.I.P. club follows.

Description of Program. The V.I.P. club offers a combination of financial and convenience products designed to meet older members' needs, augmented by a range of activities to promote social interaction and useful information. The club has been "tinkered with" every few years to fine-tune its appeal to current and potential members. Prospects for future growth are good, but accommodating a wide array of individual member interests remains a challenge.

A discount pricing strategy is in effect, reflected in the bundle of products and services offered. Members are invited to bring guests to events for an intentionally small surcharge, both as a recruitment device and as a courtesy to members.

The credit union's three locations offer in-branch services included in the product/service bundle, such as money orders and photocopies. Other benefits arrive in the member's mailbox, including the *Cruising Power* newsletter, and the MEMBERS Prime Club magazine, *Prime Times*®. Activities give the members, many of whom were co-workers before retiring from CUNA & Affiliates or CUNA Mutual Group, a welcome opportunity to socialize.

How It's Promoted. The newsletter is the main vehicle for promoting the club's activities. Flyers, postcards, and telephone calls also stimulate attendance. A call marketer uses the MCIF and records of attendance at previous events to invite members to upcoming ones.

Like Dupaco Credit Union, CUNA Credit Union is aggressive in promoting itself in local media. Television, print, radio, and billboards are all used to increase awareness of CUNA Credit Union. "There hasn't been a promotional push for club membership in the last few years," says Crowe. "The focus has been on maintaining the club's activities."

The CUNA Credit Union Objective. CUNA Credit Union will continue fine-tuning the club product to suit evolving needs of its members, and to take advantage of opportunities for increased relationships via financial planning and investment services.

"We know we have opened 360 new memberships this year. We know that 39 percent of them have our credit card; on average they have 4.3 accounts, and use an average of three services. We know from the numbers that they're likely to have share checking, money market funds, share certificates, and retirement accounts."

Crowe is exploring the credit union's MCIF data on V.I.P. Club members in search of "the *next* product they'll need."

TINKERING WITH THE MATURE MARKET PROGRAM

No one can offer you a "one-size-fits-all" recipe for your mature market program. Banks have typically focused more on discounted product bundles than on activities like Dupaco's and CUNA Credit Union's clubs. Many credit unions have relied on discounted products as well, lacking the resources or the member interest necessary to build a dynamic older members' club. But clubs offer credit unions an ideal opportunity to differentiate themselves from other financial institutions. Our credit union philosophy of "people, not profit" quite naturally finds expression in the activities and services a club can offer.

> *No one can offer you a "one-size-fits-all" recipe for your mature market program.*

Claim Your Position

Your credit union must decide whether your mature market program is weighted toward group activities or toward individual member benefits. We've

A typical bank's mature-segment product

Requirement to join: Must be age 55-plus and maintain a $500 balance in a specified checking account.

Benefits of membership:

- Special no-fee checking account
- Discounts on certain products, such as groceries or prescriptions
- Free check printing
- Free traveler's checks and money orders
- Accident, life, or other insurance
- Newsletter
- Financial/investment advice

What's missing? The people!
Credit unions enjoy an affinity relationship with their members that banks can't buy.

arrived at where the rubber meets the road—where tactics are chosen to meet objectives.

The design of your program must take its inspiration from your organization's personality—which to a large extent is given to you by your members, your management, and your image in the community at large. It's the cumulative achievement of your credit union's life as an institution. Marketers call this concept **positioning.** Differentiating yourself from competitors is the key goal of positioning.

Many factors help create your positioning:

- the tone of your marketing communications
- your members' experiences with you
- the types of people within your field of membership
- things members say about you
- things employees say about you
- your projected image of members
- the appearance of personnel and public areas
- your civic and social affiliations

It's best to take a proactive approach, choosing a positioning strategy and communicating it consistently. It's logical that your mature market program should reflect the personality of your organization as a whole—and that personality should be nurtured through your strategic marketing decisions.

Positioning as a concept has been around in one form or another since the 1950s. **Branding** has emerged as the latest extension of the positioning concept.

Positioning Defined

Positioning: a communication strategy that helps individuals identify what is unique about their organization. Positioning emphasizes those attributes in which they excel when compared to other competitors.

Credit Union Brands. A brand consists of the associations and expectations that consumers think of when exposed to a name, or a logo, or a product. Your brand brings your credit union to life in the mind of the public, communicating and demonstrating your value to them. Your brand is the vehicle that delivers your position.

Marketers have found many ways to communicate their brands. They have used brand characters and celebrity spokespeople, or have adopted a style and tone in their advertising that becomes recognizable over time.

Each credit union, in each community, occupies a strategic position and creates for itself a brand identity. Unlike banks and other financial institutions, credit unions enjoy a unique marketing opportunity: we can link our local brands with the national credit union brand. Like an umbrella sheltering the individual credit union brands, there exists a national "mega-brand" born of the credit union movement itself. National branding efforts, like that of the National Credit Union Brand Campaign, created by CUNA & Affiliates in 1999, translate into local awareness of the credit union movement and its benefits to consumers. Through national branding efforts, we use the power of collective action to build awareness of the credit

---

Successful Brands Are Built to Last

The mental associations that give a brand symbolic weight take time to develop. Once you've begun to communicate your brand, be consistent and allow it to build. The result will be as solid as your bricks and mortar.

---

union difference. Such campaigns educate consumers about the fundamental uniqueness of credit unions as financial cooperatives. National branding initiatives are designed to fuel individual credit unions' growth, on the principle that *all of us* is better than *each of us.* For a deeper discussion of branding, both local and national, consult *Credit Union Branding: Winning Strategies for Marketers,* a CUNA CPD/CUNA Marketing Council publication. Ordering information is in the back of this handbook.

Mature Market Programs and Promotions

Our discussion in this chapter has focused on the design of a product/service bundle tailored to meet the unique needs of your older members. This is a widely used method to increase the value of their relationship with you. Ultimately, the goal is increased member retention and improved member service.

Figure 4.1 lists potential services to offer through your mature market program, courtesy of MEMBERS Prime Club. Choose those that offer opportunities to illustrate your credit union's position.

As mentioned before, no two mature market programs are, or should be, exactly alike. Let your members provide input in creating the components of your program. They'll guide you in the choice of emphasis—financial benefits, social opportunities, or other enhancements. It's quite possible you may create several programs pinpointing niches within the mature market. For example, a pre-retirement planning club could serve the needs of primes, while an activities club provides outings of interest to seniors and many still-active elders, who have more leisure time.

Your tactics for serving the mature market need not, and should not, stop with the creation of a seniors' club, however! What about your primes? Your elders? Your marketing strategies should include promotions designed to offer products and services customized to fit the primary subgroups.

Lending Products. A sizable number of your older members may still be looking for loans. As baby boomers move into the mature market, the proportion of matures seeking loans will rise dramatically. Get ready for it now by developing tactical loan products, especially for your primes. These might include:

- vehicle loans
- credit cards

Figure 4.1 Potential Mature Member Services

Checking/Share Drafts
free demand-deposit account
free check printing
free traveler's checks
free money orders

Savings and Investments
share savings account
certificates of deposit
direct deposit
brokerage services

Credit Services
credit card
debit card
personal line of credit

Insurance
free accidental death and
    dismemberment
Medicare supplement
long-term care
auto and homeowners

Educational Programs
retirement planning seminars
local speakers on consumer, health, tax
    issues, and related topics
newsletter

Discounts
prescription pharmacy services
eye wear
restaurants
theaters
local retail stores

Travel
day trips to local and regional attractions
cruise or vacation packages
hotel and car rental discounts
emergency message service

Personal Services
free photocopies
notary public
safe-deposit box
credit card registration
valuable document registration
household inventory registration

Source: MEMBERS Prime Club

- home equity lines of credit
- signature loans for a variety of personal uses (travel, computer, debt consolidation)
- reverse mortgages

Savings Products. Many of your older members have savings and investments with other institutions. Why not ask them to bring these assets to their trusted credit union partner? Older members' deposits with you provide the base for loans to younger members. Appeal to matures' natural penchant for saving with a generational appeal. Design special share accounts for grandparents to share with grandchildren. Emphasize the "people helping people" philosophy, and the safety and competitiveness of your deposit products.

Educational seminars are an ideal way to help older members see the wisdom of sheltering their share accounts under the credit union umbrella. Many seniors in your membership, especially women, have paid little attention to their savings plans in the past. Services and products that help them "catch up" will be beneficial both to the members and to the financial institution that serves them so well.

Calling All Lapsed Members

As you plan your marketing tactics for your prime, senior, and elder members, keep this in mind: One out of every three nonmembers *was once* a credit union member. Ideally your marketing plan will include at least one nonmember recruitment strategy. Let's get those lost sheep back in the fold!

YOUR IMPLEMENTATION STRATEGY

At this point in the planning process, you should be gaining a clear picture of your positioning/branding strategy, your mature market program, and your promotional strategies directed to each of the primary subgroups—primes, seniors, and elders.

All that's left is to hone those strategic decisions into tactical steps required for implementation. These tactical steps will include a creative approach, an advertising media plan, and a budget.

Mature Market Creative Approach

Implementation requires the development of a creative approach. Successful member communications require creative expressions that appeal to the target audience, while reinforcing the overall positioning of the organization. The

---

approach you choose guides the look and tone of your marketing communications, from advertising to brochures to lobby posters.

The creative approach turns your marketing tactic into a compelling presentation of an idea. An excellent example is a public service TV spot that aired in the 1990s. It features an egg frying while a narrator intones, "This is your brain. This is your brain on drugs." That's a compelling presentation. It stops the audience and holds attention by dramatizing the subject—in this case with negative imagery. Your own communications will no doubt dramatize more positive aspects of your message. How that drama is achieved—whether through demonstrations or storytelling, through words or pictures—is your strategic choice.

Chapter 5 explores different methods of getting your message to your target market, and chapter 7 addresses leveraging what we know about the subsegments within the mature market to design creative approaches to communicate with them.

Mature Market Advertising Media Plan

Your tactical marketing plan will need an advertising media plan for disseminating your message. The media plan should include a mix of advertising vehicles—chosen for their ability to give you access to the right target audience, in a way that supports your positioning and creative approach.

Most credit union media plans call for only one or two advertising vehicles at a time. A typical mature market media plan for promoting a financial planning seminar might consist of flyers included with statements mailed to your older members, supported by advertisements in a local "mature lifestyles" weekly newspaper to reach nonmembers. Not surprisingly, each media plan raises scheduling considerations. When will the ads appear, and when will planning and production of the advertising components take place? A strong tactical implementation plan will include timelines detailing responsibilities and interim deadlines.

Mature Market Budget

Your tactical marketing plan requires a budget detailing projected costs and return on investment. A mature members' club needs a budget for its activities. The club's product/service bundle, especially if it features discounted products or waived fees, will have an impact on overall return on investment. This impact must be justified and planned for. Any promotional program will require a budget for advertising or other expenditures.

As you prepare your mature market program budget, discuss its impact on the overall business-unit budget with your marketing peers and manager(s).

Measuring Effectiveness. Your tactical marketing plan is not complete, however, if it lacks a means of measuring its effectiveness. As discussed in chapter 3, you must set benchmarks for performance, document your results, and analyze your findings to fine-tune your future plans.

The Marketing Plan Document

In the last chapter the importance of a *written* marketing plan was stressed. The inputs to such a plan, and the means of gathering them, were discussed. It's time to turn our attention to the writing of the plan. Writing a plan has a way of making you:

- focus on overall business strategies;
- bring others—senior management, members, staff—in on the process;
- help to project and justify expenses;
- define any necessary steps for implementation; and
- commit to a means of evaluating results.

Together these effects create a synergy you wouldn't want to do without.

What does a marketing plan look like? Each plan is as distinctive as the business it's written for. The plan document should include some or all of the following topics:

- objectives
- situation analysis
- review of internal and external marketplace issues
- statements of strategies (include marketing mix analysis)
- implementation plans
- promotion/advertising plans
- budgets and timelines
- means of evaluation and control

The plan should reflect the mission of your organization, and the preferences of your management. Above all, it should in every way be designed to serve the needs and desires of your members.

MARKETING ONE-TO-ONE (ALMOST)

To the extent that your resources permit, the marketing plan for your program should include multiple target marketing strategies to selectively address primes, seniors, and elders. We've characterized these three subgroups by age, life stage, and generational cohort.

Simply targeting groups by age brackets is useful as far as it goes, but fails to pinpoint the needs and attitudes of individuals with enough precision to break through the general roar of marketing messages around them. Further differentiating those age groups by applying our understanding of life stages and generational peers, helps us speak more directly to groups of individuals who share common ground.

We've seen that individuals' values and attitudes will, for the most part, be in tune with their generational peers' unique perspective. Individuals' needs and desires will, likewise, be predictable by the life stage they are experiencing.

Individuals' needs and desires will be predictable by the life stage they are experiencing.

By studying these factors, we come closer to understanding these niche markets *as individuals.* When we understand our members to this degree, we can be very precise in offering what each wants, when they want it. And that's a recipe for successful marketing.

In some highly technological future, not too distant in time, it will be possible—and desirable—to have individual marketing strategies matched to each and every member. In the meantime, we can prepare for that one-to-one future by leveraging what we know about primes, seniors, and elders to better serve and communicate with them.

CREDIT UNION ACTION STEPS

- Review the mature market programs profiled at the beginning of this chapter. Using the same profile format, write a similar program description for your credit union. Include only what is true and in effect today.

- Brainstorm (alone or with colleagues) a list of possible enhancements for your program. Use figure 4.1 as a starting point, choosing components that fit the personality of your credit union and its members. Ask older members to suggest additional ideas.

- Write an outline for a tactical marketing plan. Use the bullet points on page 57 and the results from these Action Steps as a starting point. When you've finished this book, revisit your outline. Perhaps you will want to craft it into a complete planning document.

GETTING YOUR MESSAGE TO THE MATURE MARKET

"Marketing is not a battle of products,
it's a battle of perceptions."

— *Al Ries and Jack Trout,*
The 22 Immutable Laws of Marketing

In Caribou, Maine, there's not much to do outdoors in winter. Television is a popular pastime in this community. If you flipped on your set in Caribou, you might catch a commercial for The County Federal Credit Union—and hear several mature members testify to their satisfaction with the County's convenience, competitive loan rates, and friendly service. The simple style of the commercial helps the speakers come across as honest and real. Its simple message helps position County FCU as a highly competitive financial service provider. The spot airs on a local television station—just part of a media schedule that includes broadcast, radio, and print advertising, since the credit union's field of membership is an open one.

In this chapter, we'll look at where credit unions advertise, and why. We'll focus our discussion on media that reach the mature market—and alternatives to mass media, as well.

Message Distribution Strategies. There are many avenues available to promote your services to your primes, seniors, and elders. One strategy is to use as many

---

communication vehicles as possible, to be sure you're not missing a portion of the audience you want to reach. It's not practical to use every media vehicle every time you advertise, of course, and strategic decisions must be reached regarding the fit of media to message and market. Let's examine how those decisions are made.

As you plan your message distribution strategy, a good rule of thumb is to balance tactics directed to *members* with tactics directed to *nonmembers.* It makes sense to direct cross-selling messages to your current members. Remember—it's eight to ten times easier to sell an additional service to a current member than to make the first sale to a nonmember. Even so, nonmember recruitment belongs in your strategic mix. There is a limit to how much your credit union can grow through additional business with current customers. At some point you'll need to add new members in order to grow.

Members or nonmembers, how should you get your message to your market? That depends entirely on the message and the market. Will mass media advertising deliver the audience you want to reach? Is there a mass media vehicle appropriate for the message you want to communicate? Is it cost-efficient? Or will another approach, such as direct mail or your member newsletter, support your goals with better impact and greater cost-efficiency? These are the questions media planners face every day. Figure 5.1 summarizes the objectives of media planning.

Mass Media—Or Direct Mail?

In chapter 1 we discussed the mature market in terms of generational cohorts and life stages. A message about a credit union benefit that appeals to a wide range of ages and stages probably belongs in the mass media. A more targeted message, such as an announcement of a joint seniors club/youth club event, is probably best promoted through a direct mail vehicle targeted to club members only.

EVALUATING THREE MATURE MARKET PROMOTIONS

As figure 5.1 illustrates, media planning involves many strategic questions, the answers to which are highly interdependent. With so many questions and so many "if this, then that" scenarios, how can a marketer hope to achieve a solid promotional plan? Most respond by exploring "what if" scenarios.

Figure 5.1 Media Planning Objectives

Definition: Media Planning—The process of deciding to whom, when, where, and how much you will advertise; what you hope to achieve; and what you intend to spend.

WHOM . . .
. . . do you want to reach? Are you certain this is the correct target?

WHEN . . .
. . . do you want to reach them? Are you reaching them when they will not only be interested in your offering, but also be most interested in receiving your message?

WHERE . . .
. . . do you want to reach them? Do we want to reach them at home, at work, both, or elsewhere?

HOW FREQUENTLY . . .
. . . do you need to reach them? Are you reaching them often enough to make your point, yet not so often that you waste money?

WHAT MEDIA . . .
. . . provide the best environments and conditions under which to reach your prospects? Have you selected media that will enhance your message and help it stand out from the media clutter?

HOW MANY . . .
. . . do you need to reach? Are you reaching enough prospects during the specific time frame that relates to your sales promotion or planning period?

AT WHAT COST . . .
. . . do you reach your prospects? Are you spending too much to accomplish your objectives? Are you spending so little that you are in essence "invisible"? Are you spending enough not only in total, but also in each individual media vehicle so as to establish an effective presence?

Let's examine three credit union scenarios. First we'll compare the promotional objectives, examining each marketing department's choice of

- objective;
- target market;
- strategy;
- incentive offered;
- creative approach; and
- rationale.

Then we'll turn our attention to the three credit unions' media plans. We'll consider each credit union's

- media vehicles available;
- time frame;
- main thrust;
- supporting activities; and
- costs and benefits.

Let's Pretend. You are invited to participate with a hypothetical panel of judges in a hypothetical competition. The following synopses have been submitted by hypothetical credit unions hoping to win the prestigious hypothetical "Golden Prime" award for best mature market promotion. As judges, we will consider the promotional objectives, then the media strategies chosen to support them. We'll keep an eye out for effective use of generational cohorts and life stages.

The following documents have been submitted for the competition.

Promotion #1—ABC Federal Credit Union, "Free Family Reunion"

Field of membership: nationwide market of employer groups in the hospitality trade.

Promotional Objective Description
- Objective: Increase the number of youth accounts per household.
- Target market: Members of the credit union's activities club. The niche targeted is seniors who are grandparents.

- Strategy: Invite target members (grandparents) to open deposit accounts for their grandchildren. Stress importance of grandparents in teaching savings habit to youth. Publicize benefits of credit union share accounts in comparison to similar offerings by other financial institutions (better rates, member-owned).
- Incentive: Hold a drawing for a "Free Family Reunion" package. The grand prize is a trip for six to a destination anywhere in the contiguous forty-eight states. Other services for a family reunion are also included in the package— free catering, announcement mailing, and the like.
- Creative approach: Offer a special share account product for older members to open for their grandchildren. Each new account opened earns the member one entry in the drawing.
- Rationale: Many matures have money in savings vehicles elsewhere. While the product offered (a share account) is functionally available to all members, selecting the mature club as an audience allows us to tailor our message to their tastes, thus increasing our ability to break through the daily advertising clutter.

In addition, since the product itself is an account opened for the grandchild, the credit union will gain young members with a potential for a lifetime relationship including education, auto, and home loans in the future.

Promotion #2—XYZ Community Credit Union, "Women's Pre-Retirement Financial Planning Seminar"

Field of membership: a 17-county area covered under a community-based charter.

Promotional Objective Description
- Objective: Increase attendance at an upcoming retirement-planning seminar for professional women.
- Target market: Female primes 50–65, currently employed outside the home, who have one or more children.
- Strategy: Direct mail appeal. Use the MCIF to prepare a mailing list, then send a two-page letter from our female CEO. The letter will express concern that many women, while involved in their family's financial decision-making process, lack a solid understanding of financial issues and are shy about asking spouses to explain details. Also, it will point out, many women in this age bracket have considerable earnings of their own, and therefore, desire greater

understanding of financial matters. Design this seminar to help female members improve their "financial savvy" and plan for an enjoyable retirement.

- Incentive: Offer enrollment in our "Pathfinders Club" for all attendees. Waive other requirements for membership, such as high account balances.

- Creative approach: The letter emphasizes the importance to children of parents' sound financial planning—and women's roles in ensuring that sound planning takes place.

- Rationale: Begin these members' affiliation with our XYZ Mature Club and increase value of attendance at the seminar. The seminar is a valuable educational "product" in itself and a marketing opportunity. Deliver a package of information with value, true to the mission of people helping people. In the process, acquire a prospect list of our female members and potential members with demonstrated interest in services and information concerning financial planning.

Promotion #3—MNO Credit Union, "Homecoming Week"

Field of membership: Regional utility companies' employees and their families.

Promotional Objective Description

- Objective: Increase membership in "MNO-Go! Club"—our mature member activities club. Plan a nonmember recruitment strategy to balance other member cross-promotion initiatives.

- Target market: Retired employees of the gas company who were once members but chose not to continue their membership after retirement. These nonmembers are over age 62. They share a common history of MNO employment and credit union membership.

- Strategy: Involve MNO-Go! Club in a member-get-a-member drive. Use MCIF records to create a call list; recruit current members of the club to identify former coworkers on the list for personal follow-up.

- Creative approach: Develop a "Homecoming Week" theme to welcome lapsed members "home"; center it around a festive open-house event.

- Incentive: Twofold. First, encourage MNO-Go! Club members to participate by offering a bonus matched by a donation to a charity of their choice. Increase the donation in proportion to memberships garnered as a result of the club members' efforts. Second, stimulate interest among prospective members by hosting an Open House event and offering special "Homecoming" rates on savings vehicles. All accounts opened during "Homecoming Week" resulting from member referrals count toward bonuses. A final event for MNO-Go! Club members (new and old) celebrates the presentation of the charity donation.

- Rationale: Using members to recruit nonmembers. The MNO-Go! Club members enjoy their club and are its best promoters. We chose the retiree/ex-member target market group because, in the past, the company has overlooked their potential. These nonmembers "look like" many of our good members, demographically speaking, and we believe they can bring considerable deposits.

As a panel of judges, we have just reviewed the promotional objectives for three competitors. Now we'll turn our attention to their media strategies.

STUDYING THE MEDIA STRATEGIES: MESSAGES TO MARKETS

The media strategies outlined in each of these scenarios describe how the message, based on the creative approach proposed in the promotional objective description, will be delivered to its target market.

Promotion #1—ABC Federal Credit Union, "Free Family Reunion"

Advertising strategy

- Possible vehicles: To reach club members, possible vehicles include:
  - ✔ mature club's newsletter
  - ✔ in-branch promotions
  - ✔ employee group's retiree newsletter
  - ✔ statement mailing
- Time frame: Promotion covers three months from initial launch until the drawing for the contest winner.
- Main thrust: In-branch promotion and monthly statements are our main thrust; we want to reach members when they are already thinking about their money.
- Supporting activities: Articles in the ABC Credit Union member newsletter and in the ABC employees' newsletter. With additional newsletter mentions, we are likely to reach the target audience an average of six times during the contest period.
  - ✔ 3 statements
  - ✔ 3 newsletters (ours)

- ✔ 3 newsletters (employee group)
- ✔ 6 visits to branches to deposit, withdraw, or perform other transactions; exposure to in-branch promotions

A total of fifteen impressions are possible.

- Costs and benefits: Approximately 0.5 percent of our current membership of 22,000 opened an average of 1.5 new accounts. This promotion resulted in 165 new accounts. Special costs incurred included development of in-branch materials ($7,000) and the contest prize itself—a $5,000 value. Our budget of $12,000 divided by more than 165 new accounts indicated we paid $72.72 per new account. Since the accounts are opened for children, who have potential for a lifetime of credit union membership, this investment looks smart.

Promotion #2—XYZ Community Credit Union, "Women's Pre-Retirement Financial Planning Seminar"

Advertising strategy

- Possible vehicles: To reach female members 50–65 who may or may not be members of our mature club, options include:
  - ✔ credit union newsletter
  - ✔ in-branch promotions
  - ✔ community mass media advertising (reaches them, but with too much waste; too broad an audience)
  - ✔ community specialized advertising (local "senior shopper" paper)
  - ✔ statement mailings
  - ✔ special direct mail
  - ✔ mature club newsletter (goes to current mature club members, a subset of the target)
- Time frame: Promotion covers about six weeks in advance of the women's financial planning seminar.
- Main thrust: Direct mail because the appropriate audience is identifiable within our own MCIF database. The letter format presents ourselves as authoritative about the matter at hand.
- Supporting activities: Direct mail is supported by advertising in the free community weekly paper directed to older adults, and press releases to other

local media. The press releases bring inclusion in upcoming events listings and other positive media attention.

Internally, our newsletter and reminder stuffers in the statements of targeted female 50- to 65-year-old members support the promotion. We also publicized it through our mature member club, suggesting members refer their friends to attend. In-branch promotion consists of teller training to suggest attendance to likely members. From these combined activities we project we will likely reach our targeted audience three or four times during the promotional period.

- Costs and benefits: Cost includes printing and mailing of the letter, printing of the reminder statement stuffers, six ad insertions in the community older-adults newspaper, and refreshments for the seminar itself. The supporting activities do not incur direct costs.

Offering the seminar was a service to our members and its cost/benefit to us depends on valuing intangibles like member loyalty and trust in their credit union—which this promotion augments.

About 2 percent of our 2,100 members within the target audience of women members who are primes attended the event. We reached our goal of forty-two attendees drawn from the target market of female members 50–65. In addition, we gained forty-two new members for the Pathfinders Club.

Promotion #3—MNO Credit Union, "Homecoming Week"

Advertising strategy

- Possible vehicles: To reach retired employees who are lapsed members of the credit union, and who meet the age 62 minimum for club membership, options include:

To reach the potential new club members:

- ✔ MNO retirees' newsletter
- ✔ telemarketing
- ✔ special direct mail

To reach potential referrers who are now members:

- ✔ MNO-Go! Club newsletter
- ✔ announcements at MNO-Go! Club events
- ✔ in-branch promotions

- Time frame: Promotion covers about five weeks. The first four weeks are devoted to publicizing the final week of new-member-drive events. The culmination is the presentation of the charity donation based on the tally of members enrolled.

- Main thrust: Telemarketing using the MCIF to create a call list and the mature club members to answer the phones. We anticipate that members will recognize old friends and former coworkers on the list and select those for personal follow-up. Our members are enthusiastic about their club and are eager to share its benefits with their acquaintances.

- Supporting activities: We support the telemarketing with announcements in the employee group's retiree newsletter. To encourage our volunteer "call staff" we promote the member drive internally. A focus of these communications is the incentives for new member referrals—a $10 bonus for the referring member, and a $10 matching donation to charity. In addition, we have "call club" times where the members come to our call center and enjoy refreshments and socialization while making their phone calls.

- Costs and benefits: Costs are held to a minimum, because current MNO-Go! Club members provided most of the people power required. Our main sources of expenses are the member referral bonuses and matching charity donations. The total market of retired ex-members consisted of about 3,500 people who still reside in our charter area. Three percent of them enrolled in the credit union—for a total of 105 new members. The bonus/donation expense amounted to $2,100. The cost per new account was roughly $20.

THE GOLDEN PRIME AWARD RESULTS

So, who wins the award for best mature market promotion? Which of these promotions will be most successful, in your opinion?

Promotion #1. ABC Credit Union's Family Reunion Contest creates a special product offering to increase interest in a relatively ordinary product—share accounts. An incentive—the contest—is a further means of increasing interest in that product. The promotion was expensive due to the lavish grand prize, but resulted in 11,000 new youth accounts.

Assessment. Given the potential for serving these members in the future, this promotion deserves praise. Its niche-targeting strategy, and pinpointing of age (65-

plus) and life stage (grandparenting) is exemplary, as is the matching of its "Family Reunion" theme to the values of its silent generation audience.

Promotion #2. XYZ Credit Union's pre-retirement seminar for women demonstrates a combination of product and incentive in order to deliver on the credit union movement's mission of people helping people. The motive was in part altruistic, to get important information to these women who are likely to need it, at a time when their need for it is strong.

Assessment. This is a fine example of strengthening the relationship between member and credit union by positioning the credit union as an authoritative source of financial advice. The internal MCIF database was a key component in identifying the target market and addressing individuals within that market as dynamic *pathfinding* women. The promotion resulted in a qualified prospect list, garnered from the seminar attendees, who have demonstrated their interest in financial services and products. This promotion also deserves praise for employing important cost-control measures—relying on the MCIF database to narrow the mailing list and using an inexpensive letter format. The content of the seminar shows a clear understanding of a tightly defined niche.

Promotion #3. MNO Credit Union's "Homecoming Week," like XYZ's seminar promotion, makes strategic use of the MCIF. Here the credit union turns to lapsed member records on the observation that these lapsed members strongly resemble current members in demographic and lifestyle traits.

Assessment. The credit union gained 105 new members who were drawn by relationships with current members of the mature club, and are therefore likely to participate in the club's activities. The astute way this promotion leverages the social aspects of the program, and its inclusion of a charitable component, are praiseworthy.

Female primes are an oft-neglected market with special needs and desires.

If these were actual credit union promotions, each would hold a strong chance of winning our "Golden Prime" award. Perhaps XYZ CU would take the grand prize—first, for placing its emphasis on serving female primes—an oft-neglected market with special needs and desires—and second, for addressing them in a way that both affirms their uniqueness and empowers them as "pathfinders."

MEDIA PLANNING 101

What do these promotions teach us about media planning? We see a variety of media approaches, but very little mass media advertising. Most credit unions use member communication vehicles—newsletters, monthly statements, and quarterly reports are the most common means of communicating with target markets (obviously, members). Targeted direct mail, using MCIF-generated lists or rented mailing lists from outside vendors are a close second, and provide opportunities to reach nonmembers as well as current members.

> *Credit unions use a variety of media approaches, but very little mass media advertising.*

Still, it's important to understand how each medium works when it comes to reaching specific target audiences, especially by age and life stage. For example, broadcast advertising can be useful in reaching baby boomer primes, who make up a large group with a large appetite for news and entertainment. For the older generational cohorts, print vehicles like newspapers and newsletters carry more weight than broadcast advertising. Different situations demand different media plans, mixing media outlets ranging from radio to the employee newsletter.

Figure 5.2 lists the most common advertising media outlets available to credit unions.

While mass media can be expensive, it's one of the best means available for communicating with a large number of people consistently over time. Each time your ad appears in print or airs on radio or TV, hundreds of thousands of people are exposed to your message. With repeated exposures, your message begins to break through the media noise all around it, and a bond begins to form between you and your audience.

It's also important to note that even though a main thrust was chosen for media usage in each promotion, it was supported with a variety of other means chosen for their availability and efficiency.

Figure 5.2 Advertising Media Outlets

Print Media
- Consumer magazines
- Business magazines
- Daily newspapers
- Weekly newspapers
- Telephone directories

Broadcast Media
- Radio
- Cable television
- Broadcast television

Print Collateral
- Direct mail
  sales letters
  promotional mailings
  newsletters
  brochures
  statement stuffers
- Point-of-purchase displays
- Billboards
- Transit ads (taxis, buses)

Mass Media for Matures—Too Much Choice?

The range of media options available to consumers is mind-boggling. We've all experienced the frustration of "fifty-seven channels and nothing on," as the Bruce Springsteen song lyric puts it. For mature adults, many of whom came of age with a few radio stations and one or two local newspapers, the frustration of too much choice can be acute.

By 1990 every U.S. household had at least one TV set, and in 80 percent of those households a VCR sat next to the set, according to *Rocking the Ages.* Sixty-six percent of those households subscribed to cable TV. In the typical household, those TV sets are on more than six hours a day. Television has become a background accompaniment to various activities, such as cooking or homework, the way radio has been used for decades. How have the matures reacted? Eighty-one percent report they feel overwhelmed.

Boomer Primes: TV-Compatible. Television usage highlights the difference between baby boomers moving rapidly into the "prime zone" and their older counterparts. Television broadcasting came into its own just as the leading-edge of baby boomers crawled into the living room to see what was on. Their elders will never be as comfortable with the hype and hooplah of television advertising as TV-bred boomers!

That's not to say the silent and G.I. generations aren't watching TV. Older adults have incorporated television into their lives, benefiting from the electronic companionship and the convenience of up-to-the-minute news and entertainment in the home. But older matures seldom turn to television for information about products and services to purchase. They have relied on newspapers and other print media for years, and that habit is not likely to change.

Mass Audience: Surplus or Bonus?

Does mass media advertising meant for matures reach too many people outside the intended niche? No! Consider . . . each individual mature is connected to a web of relatives and friends, all looking out for each others' interests. Your advertisement in the mass media may be seen by a concerned other, who will carry your message with the weight of personal referral. Offer real solutions to real problems, and your message will hit its target.

Those (usually large) credit unions that use mass media naturally try to get the most "bang" possible for every buck. At Dupaco Community Credit Union in Dubuque, Iowa, Joe Hearn combines his media spending with sponsorship of community events. "We buy ads, and aggressively promote products and services, but I'm a big believer in leveraging your media dollars. I'll say, 'If I'm going to spend the money with you, I want you to work with me on a community project.' [Members] get the word to the community. They'll assist with the organization and execution. We've done a Coats for Kids drive, a holiday benefit movie, a community garage sale . . . Partnering has worked real well for us," says Hearn.

Other Approaches to Advertising

These include telemarketing, workplace communications, the Internet, and more. Each has its utility in selectively reaching primes, seniors, and elders.

Telemarketing. With call-center staff available to do the legwork, credit unions are finding the telephone an excellent tool for solidifying relationships with members. Phone surveys are an important way to keep tabs on member satisfaction. Member service representatives (MSRs) use the telephone to cross-sell new services to current members. Credit union marketers also use database marketing techniques to create call lists of prospective members who resemble good customers in demographic and lifestyle attributes. In each of these examples, the personal touch of a telephone call demonstrates the personal service by which credit unions distinguish themselves from other financial institutions.

Members of the Silent and G.I. generations enjoy personal contact about business matters—after all, many of them remember a time when everyone did business with their neighbors, up and down "Main Street." Calls to invite individuals to events, such as open houses and seminars, remain welcome, when approached with friendly sincerity and a sense of fun.

Workplace Communications. Workplace communications to reach matures? Aren't they mostly retired? If that's what you're thinking, remember—retirement's not what it used to be. Only 36 percent of household heads retire as soon as they reach retirement age, according to the U.S. Census Bureau and the American Association of Retired Persons (AARP). Many boomer primes will switch from full-time to part-time work. Many will embark on second careers, based on hobbies or skills nurtured along the way.

So a sizable proportion of the mature market is in the workplace—and you can reach them there. If your credit union serves employee groups, leverage your relationship with sponsor groups by taking advantage of their employee communications.

> *If your credit union serves employee groups, leverage your relationship with sponsor groups by taking advantage of their employee communications.*

Use signs on bulletin boards and in break rooms to promote credit union membership to nonmember employees. "Some of our employee groups allow us to advertise in their offices, and we take advantage of it," says Donna Zaccour, Marketing Director at Seaboard Credit Union in Jacksonville, Florida.

Today many companies use corporate intranets for employee communications. At Energy First Credit Union, whose field of membership includes employees of the region's utility companies, the gas company's intranet is a key part of the media mix. "We put ads and informational pieces on their intranet. That has worked really well. When we started we were just using it for information, like when we changed our name and when we moved into our new building. Now, when we have a special promotion going on, we'll advertise it on their intranet," explains Marketing Director Darlene Diamond.

"We're proud to be part of them, so we try not to impose on their good graces. We keep it informational for the most part, and we don't do it so often it becomes an expense to the company."

Used wisely, as in these examples, workplace communications offer a cost-effective means of reaching a specific audience. Your pre-retirement planning messages can be coordinated with employer information about retirement benefits. Think creatively about ways you can partner with your employer groups.

Employer Groups: A Communication Bridge

Credit unions that serve employer groups have a bridge to reach retirees of the employer company. Does your employer group publish a newsletter for retired employees? Offer to write a financial services column or buy an advertisement.

Internet. Older adults are a rapidly growing segment of today's Internet users. The convenience of desktop financial services is a natural fit for home-bound elders, as well as for dynamic seniors so active in their retirement that they have little time for visiting the credit union.

And soon technophile baby boomers will dominate the age 50–64 "prime zone." While statistics are sketchy, it appears that those over age 55 are among the heaviest computer users, and spend more time online than any other group. This makes sense when we consider that retired people have "home time" to explore their interests online. They're hard to count, however, because they tend to be "invisible" online—they surf their interests, not their age!

In surveys, matures have expressed concern with online security. Overcoming this concern is critical if credit unions are to promote Internet financial services to this group. Older people also express concern about the value of goods and services sold over the Internet. The implication for credit unions is that Internet offerings for matures should focus on useful information rather than attempt to close sales of new products and services.

Additional Approaches. Some other nonmedia approaches available to credit unions include the following:

- Personal referral (develop a reward program for employees and/or members).
- Both your member newsletter and your senior club newsletter are vehicles that convey your advertising and editorial messages.
- Educational seminars. This is a very cost-effective technique that's brought great results for credit unions. We'll discuss seminars further in chapter 7.
- Mature member club activities. The activities of your club provide an opportunity to speak directly to members.
- Community activities. Most likely your employees and members are great volunteers. Let local media know about your activities and positive publicity may result.

Your member newsletter and your senior club newsletter are vehicles that convey your advertising and editorial messages.

Each of the means of communicating we've discussed has its own role in the media mix. Each has its own strategic impact in reaching the niche you want—be it silent generation women experiencing singlehood, or G.I. generation retirees who want health information. Consider including two or three approaches in your promotion. As the examples in the "Golden Prime" competition presented earlier demonstrate, a main thrust should be supported with a variety of other means of getting your message to market.

EFFICIENT USE OF MEDIA

Efficient use of media requires a strategic plan. Review your commitment to adequate research, planning, and follow-through, as you lay your plans.

Importance of Research. Your choice of media—and your choice will most likely include several media outlets—must be based on solid information about your current and prospective members' media habits. Whether you use a member survey, a focus group, or other market research tool, make sure you gather information before you make advertising placement decisions. Find out what your target audience reads, sees, responds too—then be there with your message.

Work to a Plan. Your advertising strategy will be more successful if you make a plan and stick to it. Use media cost comparisons and other budgeting tools to guide your strategic decisions. CUNA CPD's MERIT module 27, *Managing Advertising Guidelines,* is a good source of credit union-specific information on media planning.

Evaluate Your Results. There's a saying, "Insanity is doing the same thing and expecting a different result." It is critical that you establish benchmarks for performance, and track results against those benchmarks. Compare your predictions to your actual performance. In this way, you can fine-tune your activities to focus on those that produce the most results at the best cost efficiency.

From Mass Media to One-to-One? According to CUNA's *Marketing By the Numbers,* 40 percent of credit union's marketing budgets typically go toward newsletters—a comfortable halfway point between mass media and individual contact. Consider: Might you, with today's desktop publishing technology, be able to produce more newsletters, tailored to pinpoint more niches, within your credit union's mature market?

An effective media plan for your credit union will explore a spectrum of communication techniques, making the best strategic choices.

CREDIT UNION ACTION STEPS

- Ask members of your over-50 submarkets to bring you the contents of their mail boxes. Study the direct mail they receive. Does the competition address those markets selectively? Do you? How can you make your message stand out from the clutter?

- Get rate cards from each advertising vehicle you are considering. Make cost comparisons. Make aesthetic comparisons.

- Inventory your resources. Educational programs, newsletters, statement mailings, seminars—how can you leverage these activities for maximum impact?

RETAIL MARKETING MATTERS

"When it comes to customer service, it's the front line that counts. No doubt about it! . . . But what sparks the front line is the obvious (even if your vision is 20/200) obsession for doing it right, making it right for the customer . . ."

— *Tom Peters,* Circle of Innovation

Retail marketing matters with the mature market. Why? Because appearance counts. Your older members may come in wearing jogging suits today, but in their youths they lived in a more formal world. They wore ties or gloves when visiting their financial institutions. Older people are more aware of the grace that a little courtesy and thoughtfulness brings to daily life. How your credit union treats its older members matters. How you look—both outside and inside—and how your staff interacts with older members are factors that combine to make an overall impression.

Competition for older members is thriving in the for-profit financial services sector. Retail marketing offers you the opportunity to improve your position relative to your competition.

Retail Marketing Defined. Retail marketing is where credit union and members meet. The experience your customers receive from their interactions with your staff and facility is a result of your retail marketing efforts. Your retail marketing strategy reflects the choices you've made to distinguish your business from competitors.

The primary function of retail marketing is to bring goods and services to the customer. Retail marketing includes displaying, advertising, and promoting your products, while servicing your members.

The primary function of retail marketing is to bring goods and services to the customer.

In the retail marketplace, shoppers are becoming incredibly sophisticated. In response, retailers are honing their ability to make the shopper's experience pleasurable. In turn, shoppers have become accustomed to receiving services and products increasingly tailored to their needs. They have come to expect that shopping will be a gratifying experience, and will quickly reject retail environments that compromise that expectation. With each passing year, your members are coming through your doors with increasingly higher expectations of service.

Credit unions have long prided themselves on putting members first. But service has become one of the main factors by which competitors differentiate themselves. Now "excellent service" is claimed by just about everyone. To maintain our edge, credit unions must find new ways to excel in service. Retail marketing is the key to doing so.

SUPPORTING THE NEEDS OF *ALL* MEMBERS

"We're special in certain ways, but we don't like to be singled out," is the feeling expressed by many older people. Marketers often make the mistake of turning off potential customers by unintentionally sending the wrong message. According to a survey by Georgia State University's Center for Mature Consumer Studies, 75 percent of matures are dissatisfied with marketing efforts directed toward them. To more accurately hit the mark, it is best to think of your older members as vibrant and diverse individuals who happen to share an attribute of greater life experience.

Phil Tschudy, executive director of MEMBERS Prime Club (formerly National Association for Retired Credit Union People), suggests that, when planning marketing directed to older members, "Take off at least fifteen years. Most older people think of themselves in terms of cognitive age rather than chronological age—that is, how old they feel, rather than how old they actually are. In most cases, they think of themselves as being ten to fifteen years younger than their actual age. They look and act many years younger than their mothers and fathers did at ages 50, 60, or 70. Talk to the person, not the birth date."

Designing your retail marketing strategy for the older generational segment, then, requires finesse. Your aim is to make members feel special, but not singled out. Special services and programs for your older members will be most widely accepted when they are designed around real benefits, rather than the coincidence of chronological age. While a seniors program, for example, obviously requires an age-specific "floor" for eligibility, the thrust of the program must hold more promise if it is to have real appeal. Relationship-building through a high level of personal service is fundamental. Designing marketing efforts around generational peers is a way to deliver a high level of service.

Seaboard Credit Union—A Retail Marketing Leader

Retail marketing aimed at different generational segments was a major focus of Seaboard Credit Union in Jacksonville, Florida, when it designed its new 17,000-square-foot main office. This credit union, with $119 million in assets and 20,000 members, serves a nationwide field of membership. Even so, design of the new $4 million headquarters in Jacksonville reflects a priority placed on delighting members visiting the credit union's facility.

Three distinct demographics are targeted with three specialty clubs: the Dalmatian Club for children, the Xtra Advantage Club for teens, and the Prestige Club for matures.

Distinct areas within the credit union appeal to and serve several different demographics. Three distinct demographic groups are targeted with three specialty clubs: the Dalmatian Club for children, the Xtra Advantage Club for teens, and the Prestige Club for matures.

The Dalmatian Club provides an area for children to play while parents take care of business. It features a whimsical doghouse with television and VCR. Parents appreciate the safe and fun environment. They also appreciate the club's role in exposing their children to financial services. Each Dalmatian Club member receives a personal account card. Each deposit the child makes in a Dalmatian Club account is rewarded with a colorful sticker.

The Xtra Advantage Club for teens occupies another part of the lobby and includes stations equipped with computer terminals. Members can take care of their financial needs via computer, but are also invited to play video games, access a major web browser (an employer group of the credit union), and file résumés for perusal by businesses looking to hire.

For members over 50, the Prestige Room provides a relaxing environment. Prestige Club membership also entitles them to certain benefits such as free traveler's checks, a waived-fee checking account, a $2,000 accidental death insurance policy, and a concierge to assist them. "We cater to them greatly through our lobby. We try to meet any need they have," says marketing director Donna Zaccour.

A large "showroom" area near the entrance focuses on displays of tangible products. Fixtures are easily moved to display loan promotion idea-starters such as cars, jet skis, and motorboats. When the credit union promoted home equity loans, a model kitchen was built in the showroom. The lobby display area is a marketing tool reinforcing the idea that the credit union helps members achieve their dreams.

When Seaboard Credit Union promoted home equity loans, a model kitchen was built in the showroom.

Nancy Mattox, Seaboard's CEO, is proud of the facility. "The excitement and enthusiasm a member feels when entering the space definitely sets us apart!" she says.

Prestige for Older Members. What would you see if you walked into Seaboard Credit Union's Prestige Room? "It's a separate room, not a little booth in the open. You'd see frosted glass windows, brass letters over the front door," says Zaccour. "Within it there's a private area where individuals can go with a member service representative if they'd like to speak in private. They can use the Prestige Room for anything they'd like. In the room we have a fax machine, a photocopier, a large TV with a satellite dish. A lot of our members use it. They hold their retiree meetings, or fund-raisers for their neighborhood groups, anything like that. As long as they're a member, they're welcome. That's what we built it for. Sometimes members come in here and they don't even do a financial transaction."

Seaboard CU has found a way to make older members feel special, by providing courtesy services above and beyond the norm of other financial institutions. Seaboard excels in bringing thoughtfulness to member interactions.

Concierges and Supertellers—Excelling at Personal Service

As another part of its retail marketing program, Seaboard has integrated the "superteller" concept into its new facility. "Our supertellers are trained in all areas of the credit union," Zaccour explains. "A member can sit down, open up an account, cash a check, and take out a loan, all with the same member service representative. Members don't have to wait in a teller line to cash a check, then go to the loan area for a loan officer, then go somewhere else for a share certificate. It's all sit-down, face-to-face. The seniors appreciate that."

Seaboard is not alone in using supertellers. The superteller concept is catching on with credit unions across the nation. So is a related concept, the first-impression person, or concierge. This is usually the first personal touch that members encounter upon entering the credit union.

Traditionally this person has been referred to as the receptionist. Until recently, in the typical credit union you would find a seated receptionist near the door, often occupied on the telephone, or with head down over some paperwork.

Studies have found that a person seated behind a desk appears to be less friendly than a person standing or sitting on a stool. This standing or near-standing position makes one seem poised for a friendly greeting. When customers are greeted within ten feet of the entrance, by someone who is clearly intent on helping them, they tend to perceive the establishment as warm and friendly. You have probably seen this retail wisdom in effect in your local stores.

Credit unions are taking advantage of this knowledge by placing a first-impression person, or concierge, on a stool behind a counter-height station, or simply standing, near the door. For similar reasons, teller lines are moving toward the rear of lobbies, to lessen the unfriendly impact of the sight of anonymous backs waiting in lines.

While the traditional receptionist stayed in one place most of the day, today credit union roving concierges move about the lobby making sure everyone's needs are served. For example, the concierge might show members how to use ATM machines or how to make transactions online.

It's not hard to see how supertellers and concierges help older members feel well-served when visiting their credit unions.

Vista FCU Emulates Disney Guest Service. For Vista Federal Credit Union in Burbank, California, being the employee credit union for the Walt Disney Company has resulted in retailing ideas borrowed from one of the world's great marketers. Disney stores were among the first to use greeters in the retail environment, and Vista FCU has taken a page from their parent company's book. "The Disney expectation of service is so much higher. We have to emulate their guest service," notes Jeff York, vice president of marketing.

"One of the things we've noticed is that our lobbies would be clogged with people, to the point where you couldn't even see inside. So we've done a total reconfiguration of our main branch at Disney. We put the tellers all the way in the back, and 'retailed' the environment in the front. We have a greeter like in the Disney stores. That person helps with keeping the lobby organized and friendly. We've got "Enlighten" videos playing. We've got self-service kiosks, places to sit down and use the Internet, right in our lobby. Now it's more open to people. Older members are more apt to come in and take advantage of the products and services when there aren't visible waiting lines."

> *"Older members are more apt to come in and take advantage of the products and services when there aren't visible waiting lines."*

Imagine what would make the transaction experience delightful for members of every age and life stage, from youth to elder. Design those concepts into your service delivery via retail marketing. The result will be increased competitiveness. In the end, you help deliver on the universal credit union promise of superior member service.

MAKING RETAIL DESIGN CHOICES THAT SUPPORT OLDER MEMBERS

Within your retail environment are fixtures, printed materials, and physical arrangements that, by their design, improve or worsen your older members' experience of your facility. As a marketer, you can recommend design choices that are appropriate for your matures who are elders, for example, without stigmatizing them as "aged" or "feeble." It's simply a matter of consideration.

The experiences of Vista FCU and Seaboard CU are just the tip of the iceberg. As these examples show, rearranging lobby space so that teller lines are located out of immediate lines of sight, and providing helpful greeters and service people, are changes that make for a more pleasant and welcoming experience for all members.

Another operational feature that helps older members interact with the credit union is the presence of a call center. At Energy First Credit Union in Monterey Park, California, Director of Marketing Darlene Diamond relates her experience. "We have a really active call center. They can help you with just about any transaction you want to do. We also have our audio response system—the Credit Union Phone Information Device, or 'CUPID.' But the seniors prefer the call center. They like to talk to a person. That's great for cross-selling. That's what our phone center people are trained to do."

Encourage Your Guests To Bring Guests

Older adults tend to shop in groups, typically as couples. Providing them with comfortable seating, and complimentary snacks and beverages, are ways credit unions let members know their guests are welcome.

Take a Fresh Look. To get an idea of the retail design choices affecting your older members, try looking at your facility from their perspective. Ask a few older individuals to accompany you on a walk through the credit union. Pretend you are entering for the first time. What do you notice? What elements of the environment might present unintended obstacles to older members' enjoyment of the experience?

Concern for safety is not strictly an age-related factor. That said, research has shown that security—physical, psychological, and financial—is a primary concern among adults aged 50-plus. Your choice of lighting, landscaping, and location contribute to your members' perception of physical security when doing business with you.

Simple changes to accommodate the needs of diverse members might include wider aisles and looser seating arrangements, for example. Young mothers with strollers and shoppers with packages will likely appreciate these considerations as much as will elders in wheelchairs. Remember: Age is not the issue—accommodation of diverse needs is the goal.

While you're in the lobby, consider the printed material you see. Ask your older guests for feedback on your signs, brochures, and application forms. Should the type be bigger? Are the colors clear, distinct, and pleasing to older sensibilities? Your "generation X" loan promotion doesn't have to please your seniors club members, of course. Still, the overall impression of printed material in the lobby can affect your members' experience.

OFFERING OPTIONS FOR MEMBERS WHO VALUE CONVENIENCE

For all members, but especially for older members, a visit to the credit union can be a social event. Members enjoy encountering neighbors, coworkers, and friends as they go about their daily errands. Can you augment this aspect of your service by offering other personal and business-support services to them?

Some of your older members are active retirees. Many credit union marketers have commented on how busy and mobile these members are. "They're always on the go," is the consensus. For these members, as well as younger busy executives and two-career couples, thoughtful conveniences are a delightful addition to member service. For other older members, health or limited mobility make the activities of daily living more cumbersome. For these members, little conveniences make a big difference.

Little conveniences make a big difference.

Most credit unions offer financial convenience services such as check cashing, money orders, and traveler's checks. But how about other conveniences that facilitate members' lives? Might your credit union offer a place to drop off dry-cleaning or charity collection items?

The Seaboard example mentioned earlier in this chapter demonstrates the popularity of offering older members a place to use a fax or copier, to watch television, and to hold meetings. Reports indicate that as baby boomers retire, many will be actively involved in entrepreneurial activities, such as home-based businesses.

Many will also spend considerable time maintaining their investment portfolios. Could you set aside a room for these adventurous boomers to use as they pursue their interests?

Services traditionally thought of as "business support" will be more in demand as boomer primes cross the threshold into retirement. Access to business equipment, to financial news and information, and to the Internet will be important to these members. When you provide these services, you solidify your personal relationship with them. When you're a valuable part of their daily routines, you're unlikely to be easily replaced by other competitors.

Marketing Internet Convenience

With every passing month, more matures are accessing the Internet. This affects your retail marketing to older members in two ways.

Your older members may need help keeping up.

Experience has shown that older members prefer to approach technology through people. In other words, they like to be personally shown how to use new tools in safe, sociable, nonthreatening situations. Then, and only then, are they likely to use the new technology on their own. Some credit unions have successfully paired teens with older members in productive intergenerational Internet sessions. Whether you choose to involve teens, rely on your Information Technology department, or call on other resources, you stand to benefit when you help your senior members build Internet skills.

Your matures will appreciate home financial services' convenience.

Whether your older members are so active they're never home, or so limited by circumstances they rarely leave it, they are likely to appreciate the Internet's ability to deliver financial services anywhere. True to their generally conservative attitudes, matures aren't showing a willingness to just plug in their credit card numbers and go nuts over the Net. Still, once security concerns have been allayed, older individuals are among the groups who stand to benefit most from the convenience and flexibility offered by Internet financial services. Help them overcome security concerns to experience the Internet's benefits and see trust build.

Adaptations to Serve Your Older Members

Credit union marketers who are sensitive to the changing physical needs of older adults will be better positioned to serve this valuable member segment.

Visual displays, customer service interactions and environmental design may all need to be adapted to accommodate any deficits in function that aging may bring.

With regard to vision changes, the marketing department can take the lead in making the facility friendly to those of all abilities, with improved signage, lighting, graphic design, and color applications.

For improved customer service interactions, consider developing a training program to help your member service staff relate to the experience of their older customers. Coach frontline people to speak directly, clearly, and evenly. Their control of vocal pitch, rate of speech, inflection, and volume, might be the factor that determines whether an older member's experience is pleasant or frustrating. The training you provide and the standards you set for appearance, professionalism, and listening skills have tremendous impact when it comes to pleasing older members.

EMPHASIZING COMMUNICATION SKILLS TO SERVE OLDER MEMBERS

Most members would agree that knowledgeable and enthusiastic employees are vital when it comes to good service. But the ability to communicate effectively depends on more than knowledge and enthusiasm. Generally, good member service people possess two basic qualities: empathy, and the ability to listen.

Frontline Staff Should Be Aware of Generational Personalities

Consider briefing your frontline member service staff on the generational cohorts described in this series, *Marketing Across the Generations*. Knowing more about other individuals' life experiences will increase your staff's ability to empathize—and to serve.

Consider hiring older individuals in member service positions. Many are interested in flexible or temporary work, an advantage for you as an employer. Your credit union will benefit from their enthusiasm and loyalty. Another benefit: They've experienced most of life's stages!

The ability to listen well is a life skill that we all would do well to master. Listening has tremendous psychological value. Make sure training is available to member service staff to help them become better listeners.

Let staff know it's okay to take the time to serve older members well. All mature members should be encouraged to talk about themselves. How do they feel? What sorts of activities are they involved in? What are their opinions of various products and services you offer? Ask staff to watch for both cross-selling opportunities and useful feedback.

Good listening skills are vital if member service people are to understand each older member's personal needs and concerns. When empathy and listening are matched with extensive product knowledge, member service staff can live up to the credit union promise of people helping people.

How May I Help You?

Most of your older members are working and playing as hard as ever. Don't assume they are "slowing down." Rather, assume their active lives produce financial needs for which you can become a trusted resource. "How may I help you?" is more than a catch phrase—it's the key to growing member relationships.

Train and Communicate. As we saw in chapter 4, Dupaco Community Credit Union's Prime Time Club places an emphasis on activities, including everything from local charity events to overseas travel. SVP Joe Hearn recognizes the importance of staff training in maintaining good relationships with older members. "The frontline staff is critical. They do a great job with older members, making them feel wanted."

At Dupaco, a part-time senior coordinator plans and executes the club's activities, with support from the marketing department and the member service staff. That makes good communication between departments critical. "The marketing department sends out the newsletter, so we know what's going on, and the senior club coordinator knows what's going on, but we've got to make sure the frontline staff knows what's going on," Hearn explains. "An older member's going to be in here making a deposit, and say, 'Oh, by the way, what about that trip?' Who does the teller go to when a member has a question? Communication is important. You can never communicate enough."

RETAIL MARKETING MAKES A DIFFERENCE

When it comes to strategically targeting older members for your marketing efforts, retail marketing has impact. A review of your retail marketing strategy may reveal opportunities for operational changes that could result in improved service to all members—not just your older submarkets. Concierges, supertellers, and special market-specific retail zones within the credit union are examples of operational changes to serve members better. Because of their emphasis on personalized service, these changes are highly recommended for improving relationships with older members.

The Member Service Moment. The physical environment is only part of your members' experience of your credit union, however. Within it, the drama of customer interaction is taking place. By working with your member service manager(s) and training department, you can help shape that drama into a delightful experience for older members. Your goal should be to create memorable member service moments.

Training in empathy and listening will help young staff members be pleasant and respectful with matures. Training in cross-selling technique will help them serve those members better, while helping your credit union attain sales goals.

Personal service is a big draw for matures.

Personal service is a big draw for matures. And yet, the financial services industry is focusing on reducing face-to-face contact with customers as a means of controlling costs. Teller-based services, admittedly, are more expensive to provide than automated transactions via ATMs and telephones. How should credit unions balance the efficiency of automation with the friendly service only people can provide?

The simple reality is, a trip to the credit union is a social opportunity. Members look forward to seeing familiar staff members and running into friends and neighbors as they visit. Encourage them to enjoy this socially vital experience.

The bottom line: your credit union is an essential part of your older members' lives. Take control of the aspects you can improve to deliver a gratifying experience to those valued customers. Then welcome them—your member/owners.

CREDIT UNION ACTION STEPS

- Review whether a superteller, first-impression person, or concierge is an appropriate operational model for your credit union. Why or why not? Who has the authority to make such a decision? What is their "take" on it? Hold a brown-bag discussion group with appropriate people from senior management.

- Invite a few older members to walk through the credit union with you. Solicit their input on the physical environment, both external and internal. Take a tape recorder with you, and capture their comments. Review these with your marketing staff and facilities manager.

- Try moving about your credit union in a wheelchair or with a walker. To augment the experience, add ear muffs and sunglasses. What improvements does this "trial run" suggest to you?

- Draw a grid with seven rows and four columns, as shown here. Ask your member service staff to call to mind specific members who fit these various categories, and write their names in the appropriate squares on the grid. Ask what is known about these members. What specifics do you know about their lifestyles? In what ways do they resemble our descriptions of primes, seniors, and elders? In what ways do they differ from commonly held stereotypes of older people? Let these people serve as reminders not to "pigeon-hole" your members by age.

Market segment (Age)	Middle adult (50–64)	Late adult (65–79)	Elder (80–plus)
Empty nest			
Caregiver			
Grandparent			
Singlehood			
Retirement			
Second career			

LEVERAGING WHAT WE KNOW ABOUT THE MATURE MARKET

"If your business has been targeting the over-50 market for some time, you've been enjoying your golden years. Once the baby boomer generation enters the market, everything will change—from the market's sheer size to the dynamics at work. Every industry will have to rethink its product offering and the way it markets."

—*Mike Ogden*, Dallas Business Journal

Previous chapters of this book have attempted to characterize three major subgroups within the mature market, give you a sense of what those unique segments mean to credit unions, and suggest how you can go about marketing selectively to them—for their benefit and your credit union's. At this point, we hope, you are feeling armed and ready to commence a mature market program. If that's the case, what is left to be said?

This concluding chapter is geared not toward helping you get started, but toward helping you go further.

While we have tried throughout the *Marketing Across the Generations* series to present accurate insights and recommendations for the immediate future of generational marketing, we are taking aim at a moving target. Each generation, as it ages, brings its own unique cohort identification to each life stage—core values, attitudes, motivators, and needs particular to it alone. The assumptions and lessons we've learned from marketing to the previous cohort will have to be re-examined again and again as new cohorts move into new life stages.

In this chapter we will first look at your relationship with the older members of the 50-plus population—the seniors and elders who have, for the most part, retired from the workforce.

Then, we'll turn our focus to the primes—those "young matures" who more resemble their younger brothers and sisters in the baby boomer cohort than their elders. The primes will be dominated by their tremendous energy to redefine both the "when" and the "how" of traditional transitions from work to retirement. "Longer life was the twentieth century's greatest gift," states Gary Becker in *Business Week*. ". . . Life expectancy, as well as the quality of life at older ages, will continue to improve rapidly during the next few decades." Futurists like Becker foresee an alert, active older population—one that presents a huge opportunity for alert credit union marketers to both win new members and serve underserved markets. Everything you know about marketing to matures will be redefined as the primes age.

SENIORS ARE READY FOR MEMBERSHIP: ARE YOU WELCOMING THEM?

The mindset of many seniors and elder retirees is a natural match with the credit union philosophy—in part because the movement was built by them. Their values of loyalty, conservatism, and service have become values of the credit union movement itself. Those members who contributed to the growth of credit unions have, through their hard work, earned hoped-for years of rich and full retirement. They look to their financial institutions to help them make wise choices, so they can collect that reward. These people deserve to be credit union members. Have you welcomed them in?

Membership Access

As we know, in recent years credit unions' competitors have chosen to make membership access a battleground in Congress—part of the ongoing effort to challenge credit unions' tax-exempt, nonprofit status.

Thanks to intensive efforts by credit union supporters, the Credit Union Membership Access Act (CUMAA) was signed into law in August 1998. Early in 1999 new, more liberal, field of membership policies for federal credit unions went into effect. Any federal credit union may now choose to adopt a more restrictive definition than that described in the Act, but no federal credit union may establish a more expansive definition.

Because of these recent changes, your credit union may have recently re-examined its membership policy. Are you familiar with current guidelines as they apply to seniors who live in your community, or those who are related to your current members?

Review Your Charter—and Your Communications. As a marketer, it's a good idea to review your charter and bylaws from time to time, to make sure you understand who is eligible to join the credit union. What is your credit union's current policy regarding membership? If your definition is more restrictive than the CUMAA guidelines, what is the reasoning behind the restriction? Have your board and senior management considered expanding the credit union's membership policies? Senior family members may become eligible under a broadened definition. Since these people hold considerable sway within their families regarding financial matters, they often become strong advocates for credit union membership to others in their extended families. If you have restrictive policies, they may be closing the door to desirable new member relationships.

> *Since senior family members hold considerable sway within their families regarding financial matters, they often become strong advocates for credit union membership to others in their extended families.*

Review your marketing materials and member communications as well. If your definition was more restrictive in the past, but has been broadened in the meantime, it's quite possible that members are not aware of your new policy.

Energy First Credit Union in Monterey Park, California, found itself in this situation. As Director of Marketing Darlene Diamond explains: "Our single sponsor has always been utility workers and their families—a very 'pure' membership by today's standards. Until recently, the family membership was limited to spouses and children under age 18. A year and a half ago, we opened that up. Now parents of members can join, and children can continue as members even when they're grown."

The change in membership policy created a communication issue. Diamond describes her predicament: "We tell the members over and over that their family members are welcome to join. But you can ask a member on any given day, and they're likely to say they didn't know that."

Your members' understanding of your policies builds gradually, over time. Their perception of who may or may not be eligible for membership comes as a result of your written communications via newsletters and annual reports; coverage in the news media; employer group communications; and impressions they receive directly when interacting with you.

While some might think member understanding of eligibility policies is a relatively insignificant point, you as a marketer realize it is crucial. According to the Consumer Federation of America, credit union members are the most satisfied of all financial institution consumers. Members are typically quick to share their enthusiasm for their credit union with others. Your current members represent a potential hotbed of new-member referrals. You wouldn't want misperceptions about eligibility to cool that fire.

MCIF Households

With proper data collection, your Marketing Customer Information file (MCIF) can help you segment members *and their families* by age and life stage. If you have gathered information about family members and relationships in your MCIF database, you can create a targeted address list for a direct mail piece or statement stuffer to recruit mature members.

CREATE MARKETING MATERIALS
THAT OLDER ADULTS RESPOND TO

Throughout this book, we hold to the premise that matures are not one market, but a collection of unique niche markets with particular values, likes and dislikes, diverse needs and wants.

As we age we become less, not more, alike. Teens and young adults are perhaps most alike, in that they consistently conform to fads. As we mature, we gain confidence, independence, and self-awareness. We no longer care about conformity. By the time we reach the older-adult life stages, we are quite aware of our uniqueness—and much less likely to respond to mass marketing appeals.

> *As we mature, we gain confidence, independence, and self-awareness.*

This strongly suggests that segmenting your market by age and life stage is essential when it comes to developing persuasive marketing materials.

Does this mean you need to develop entirely different materials for each niche market? No. The variations need not be dramatic, only astute. Energy First CU's Darlene Diamond has found that even slight alterations to promotions can make the message more appropriate to different generational segments. "We had a really successful home equity mail promotion last spring. We wrote one version for members under age 45, and another for older members. The message was just slightly different. With the younger group we wrote it a little more youthful, a little more upbeat," Diamond points out. "With the older group, there were slight changes in the copy. But more important, we portray them as active seniors. These aren't people in rocking chairs on the front porch. The name for our seniors group, the Hi-Energy Club, counters that stereotype."

Good Old Ways and Good Old Days. Older adults are demanding a "good feeling" about the companies and people they do business with. This attitude stems from their earlier experience of a more rural America, populated with small towns and local independent merchants. They are less impressed than younger adults by trappings of image. While they appreciate a bargain as much as anybody, they demand that their purchases reflect good value for the money.

Credit unions are well-positioned to respond to this demand. They offer good value, and as member-owned cooperatives, engender good feelings about the people involved. As the banking industry continues its course of growth through mergers and interstate operations, credit unions look better and better to individuals who want to do business with locally owned, independent institutions. The credit union philosophy fits with older adults' values.

Family at the Center. Many of today's seniors and elders overcame great challenges to achieve success. After years of work and sacrifice, they've arrived at a time in their lives when they should be reaping their rewards. However, habits of a lifetime don't change overnight. While many have reached a level of financial comfort, their style of spending has always been cautious and savings-focused. Even though we see bumper stickers saying, "I'm Spending My Kids' Inheritance," we will probably never see this generation over-indulge in spending for selfish reasons.

Throughout their lives, these individuals have been saving and spending for others—most often, their children. They believe in the importance of family. Credit unions are in a natural position to offer opportunities for intergenerational sharing. Joint activities between seniors clubs and youth clubs have proven successful for credit unions that have explored them.

> *Credit unions are in a natural position to offer opportunities for intergenerational sharing.*

"We've had joint activities," reports Dupaco Community Credit Union's Joe Hearn. "We promoted a pool party to the senior club as well as the youth club. That worked out real well. The senior club is also active in the community. We've adopted a huge garden at the local arboretum. The seniors bring their grandkids to pull weeds. There are opportunities for overlap. It makes sense. You can co-promote events, which helps your attendance."

As credit union marketers, we can celebrate the role of grandparents and great-grandparents in the lives of their families. Our newsletters, for example, might offer advice on activities for grandparents and grandchildren to do together, and create a forum for talking about ethics and values.

Enjoying Well-Earned Rewards. Core values of older adults are frugality, responsibility, and caution. You probably know one or two older members who are millionaires but still maintain the modest lifestyle of their struggling years. It's not easy to convince those in the silent and G.I. generations to live like the "idle rich"—and as their financial advisors, we wouldn't suggest it.

Still, there's a difference between caution and pointless self-denial. The pleasure taken in the purchase of a vacation home or a trip with grandchildren enriches the retirement years and increases the quality of life of older people. Deciding to spend money so "selfishly" can be difficult. We have the potential to help individuals understand their financial situations better, so they can judge when it's "okay to enjoy ourselves a little."

Leisure time, personal fulfillment, and renewed relationships with spouses and friends become motivations for these individuals. The credit union plays a role in helping them achieve these dreams, through loans and other products, through social activities, and through assistance with sound financial planning.

Persuasive Marketing Messages for the 65-Plus Set

Several key factors are important to keep in mind when marketing to senior and elder adults. Stereotypes regarding age, product usage, and diminished lifestyles and opportunities can get in our way, if we're not careful. Consider the following.

Age Isn't the Issue. If you asked a mature member to describe himself, he's not likely to start with his age. Life stage—with its focus on particular interests, concerns, and consumer needs—is more relevant to the older individual. The message you send should be tailored to a specific life stage—for example empty nesting, caregiving, or planning for an active retirement.

People naturally think of themselves as younger than they really are. Most of us look, and feel, much younger than our parents did at the same age. Mentally subtract ten years from their chronological ages when you write advertising copy directed at older members.

Portray a Positive Image. Show adults in their mature years as vital and productive. Use positive, affirming phrases like

- "Retire on your terms"
- "Take control of the future"
- "Choose your own path"
- "Your hard work is paying off"

Don't be afraid to show feelings—if done tastefully. Many older adults are happily experiencing renewed emotional lives—sharing the joy of grandchildren, getting reacquainted with spouses.

Older adults appreciate good news about their life stage. They'll respond well to messages that reflect a can-do, positive attitude. These messages are natural story material for newsletters.

Dupaco Community Credit Union, Dubuque, Iowa, does an excellent job of portraying mature members positively in its senior newsletter, *Prime Times.* Joe Hearn describes a recurring column, called the "Prime Time Profile":

"We take an individual or a couple within the Prime Time Club, and we'll profile their interests, their activities, a little bit of their background. We'll talk about how they feel about the credit union. People are interested in what other people are up to. It's a real 'feel-good' thing. We give the featured people fifty extra copies, and they pass those out to their families. We've heard stories—people they haven't talked to for years will call and congratulate them. It just resonates out there."

An example newsletter profile is shown in figure 7.1.

At Founders Federal Credit Union, a credit union for employees of companies affiliated with Springs Cotton Mills, members age 60 and older are eligible to join the Springtimers Club. Members enjoy a variety of advantages, including an upbeat newsletter. The monthly publication is filled with stories from other members, recipes, financial hints, and help. Stories on topics such as "My Most Embarrassing Moment," or "The Best Advice I Got From My Parents," bring laughter to readers.

Tell the Whole Story. Older adults are *readers.* When you present them with information, they'll read every word of copy—if it's written in a language that is straightforward, dignified, and honest. While older adults watch television as much as any generational segment, they turn to television as a source of entertainment—not product information. When it comes to evaluating products and services for purchase, they prefer print.

Figure 7.1 Prime Time Profile

Jim and Rose Marie Ryan

At one time or another we've all been told, "Don't talk to strangers." But for Prime Time Club members Jim and Rose Marie (Rosey) Ryan, talking to strangers is a vital part of helping make visitors feel like welcome guests in our community.

Born and raised in Dubuque, Rosey attended St. Anthony's Elementary and graduated from St. Joe's High School. She then enrolled in the X-Ray Technology program at The Finley Hospital, where she received her Registered Technologist (RT) designation following two years of training. "I wanted to be in a caring profession," says Rosey of her decision to work in health care.

Jim was born in rural Peosta near the monastery "with the Irish Ryans." After his early years in a one-room shoolhouse, he attended Washington Junior High and Senior High School. At Senior, he majored in vocational sheet metal—a trade he immediately took up upon graduation and has practiced for 45 years. "I'm very close to retirement," says Jim. How close? "Very close," he answers with a smile.

Married 41 years in July of this year, the Ryans first met at the Melody Mill Ballroom. They're the proud parents of a son and a daughter and were recently blessed with their first grandson.

As their children grew, the Ryans became involved in Friendship Force, acting as a host family for foreign visitors from Korea, Japan, Lithuania, and Austria. "We got involved when our kids were at an impressionable age," reveals Rosey. "We wanted to expose them to different cultures." In addition to hosting foreign visitors, the Ryans have also traveled extensively throughout the Orient and Europe.

Not ones to sit idly by, Jim and Rosey are avid bikers, averaging nearly 1500 miles of peddling each year. In the past 15 years, they've also participated in all, or portions of, the Des Moines Register's Annual Great Bike Ride Across Iowa (RAGBRAI). "We like the freedom and serenity of biking," says Rosey. "We bike a lot of backroads," interjects Jim. "There's a lot of beauty in the area we didn't know about—we just stumbled across it." But the Ryans' biking is not restricted to Iowa and the tri-state area. In the past they've also biked in Japan, and around Colorado and Ireland with their daughter and son-in-law.

For the past 15 years, Jim and Rosey have spent the winter months as ski instructors at Sundown Mountain. "I really like to teach . . . and we work with great people," smiles Rosey. Jim agrees, adding, "I like the camaraderie and enjoy the natural beauty. And you meet people from across the area and around the world."

Reprinted with permission from Dupaco Community Credit Union's *Prime Times* newsletter.

As with biking, their ski activities are not limited to the Dubuque area. The Ryans also travel to Colorado one or two times each year, and have skied in Austria.

In addition to biking and skiing, Jim maintains some land that he and Rosey own, "although I can't say I really enjoy it." he jokes. And because he readily admits he's "very close to retirement, what does the future hold? "We'd like to travel to Alaska and Australia," he reveals.

Rosey currently works as a step-on guide for the Dubuque Historical Society for which she conducts architectural, historical, and progressive dinner tours. And when the Delta Queen Riverboat docks for visits, she's there to help welcome passengers to Dubuque. "Working for the Historical Society you meet people from all over the world," says Rosey. How did she get involved working as a guide? "I was teaching educational historical programs to a lot of children and that led me into working with adults."

Credit union members for over 40 years, it was Jim's brother, employed by the Dubuque Packing Company, who first got them involved. "We really like Dupaco," says Jim.

Of the many places they've visited, do the Ryans have a favorite place? "Each place had something unique to offer—its own cultural nuance," says Rosey. "Europe was the easiest. The Far East was the most intriguing." Nonetheless, the Ryans are still glad to call Dubuque their home. "With our quality of life and friends and family in the area, we like Dubuque," says Jim. And Dubuque is indeed fortunate to have quality people like the Ryans helping strangers feel like welcome guests.

Sixty-four percent of adults over 50 agree with the statement "technology sometimes intimidates me," according to *Rocking the Ages.* So when explaining complex services or products, especially technological ones like computer financial services, focus on function and make the message friendly. Carefully review your written drafts for confusing hyperbole. Cut it—and replace with accessible, honest, familiar language.

When explaining complex services or products, focus on function and make the message friendly.

Older people aren't necessarily put off by technology, but they didn't get the chance to absorb it at an early age. They work harder to understand it, and appreciate more help in the form of better explanations, personal training assistance, and mutual support.

This is especially true when it comes to the Internet.

THE INTERNET: A NEW WORLD OF POSSIBILITIES

The Internet is increasingly popular with older adults. Web monitoring and tracking firm Media Metrix reported in 1999 that 15 percent of adults over 50 were using the Internet, up from just 5 percent in 1996. This number will undoubtedly continue to rise, as "senior-friendly" technology comes along. High-resolution monitors and applications like Web TV that use the familiar livingroom TV set will make Internet access more comfortable and less intimidating for older people.

Why Go There? Adults over 50 cite the desire to communicate with friends and family as the number one reason for buying a computer. Seniors who grew up writing letters find the Internet an effective way to keep in touch with their relatives. Grandchildren who never write letters promptly respond to e-mails.

Convenience is an important factor in drawing seniors to the Internet. Those who don't like driving at night, or dealing with crowded shopping centers, find home shopping very appealing. The ability to take care of "errands" electronically—paying bills online, or researching an interest without going out to the library, for example—are benefits of Internet access with considerable value to seniors.

Computer-Based Financial Services

The Internet brings the possibility of financial services delivered wherever a computer and modem are plugged in. Many retired people are mobile, traveling for adventure or moving between alternate northern and southern homes with the seasons. They make a promising market for debit and credit cards, auto/recreational vehicle loans, and convenience services like direct deposit and bill-paying. Any of these can be combined with Internet financial services for an attractive mature-niche product offering.

With your web site bookmarked on their browsers, your active older members are never far from a credit union branch. Credit unions have been somewhat slow to get involved with PC home financial services technology, but that tide is rapidly turning. By now it's clear that even small credit unions need to have an Internet presence. "Senior-friendly" areas of the site should include enhancements such as larger typefaces, bright colors against dark backgrounds, and special instructions and content tailored to older adults' needs.

Even small credit unions need to have an Internet presence.

Fairwinds Credit Union, based in Orlando, Florida, serves members in fifty states and some twenty-six foreign countries—in part through their excellent web site. Located at *www.fairwinds.org*, the site includes everything from rates to membership application forms to personal retirement income strategies. Members may check account balances, transfer money between accounts, pay bills online, and access an online brokerage service. The site's large library of financial articles, covering investing, insurance, and other money management topics, is popular with older members.

Matures: Choosy Surfers

Older Internet users have the time to explore the Internet, but they have little patience for jargon, or sites that are difficult to navigate. They surf their interests, including sports, health, travel, and investing—but they move on if they find a site difficult to use.

Retirees, coping with life on fixed incomes, find this kind of access to information about their financial accounts reassuring. Given their conservative conditioning, however, they're not going to be sold overnight on the wisdom of typing in personal information and access codes where they fear "just anybody can get at it." With their resistance to complicated jargon, explanations intended to dispel unnecessary concerns may just cause members to give up and conclude, "This is too complicated for me."

Credit unions will experience more success promoting computer-based services to older members when we leverage what we already know about this group.

Get Old and Young Together. Some organizations, such as churches and schools, have organized programs that bring young people and senior citizens together to explore computers and the Internet. Consider creating a program at your credit union, perhaps involving your young-adult members, or inviting grandparents to bring their grandchildren to an Internet fun-for-all time. Opportunities to spend time learning and enjoying together are appreciated. Youths share their knowledge of the Internet with their elders, while the older adult has an opportunity to teach young relatives about money skills, shopping for good values, and other life skills.

Speak Respectfully. If you use e-mail, or participate in chat groups, you've experienced the Internet style of communication. It has become accepted protocol to write in a telegraphic, truncated style. This does not go over well with the mature market, however. Hipper-than-thou terminology and in-group acronyms like IMHO only confuse and irritate older users. Your seniors and elders are used to more formal correspondence and will prefer simple, clear messages.

Develop Material for Interests, Not for Ages. Online seniors don't wear a sign proclaiming their age, nor should they. We all use the Internet to delve into topics that interest us; retired people more so, because they have the luxury of time to explore their interests. Successful sites are created around interest categories. Seniors are politically active. The Internet is ideal for helping them keep abreast of policy developments and communicate with elected officials. Help your older members connect with their own power as a social force, via the Internet—and tap their considerable influence in support of issues affecting the credit union movement.

Information and convenience are the drivers that bring these older users online, and sites that deliver information and convenience will earn their return visits. Your credit union web site should offer both.

Idea-Starters: Offer Something for All Ages and Stages

Special services aimed at seniors typically emphasize one of two approaches: financial programs or social programs.

Financial programs focus on discounted fees for convenience services, higher rates on high-balance share accounts, and waived fees for products like traveler's checks and money orders. Most seniors programs at banks take this route. Due to our nonprofit structure, credit unions are often able to offer more attractive financial packages than banks. However, given banks' larger advertising budgets, credit unions have difficulty separating themselves from the pack when they rely on financial programs to get attention.

In the social approach, credit unions provide opportunities for people to get together. Trips and outings are frequent features of such programs, as well as get-togethers for games, meals, or educational presentations. Social activities are especially popular with employer-based credit unions because of the opportunities for retired members to keep in touch with former coworkers.

> *Social activities are especially popular with employer-based credit unions because of the opportunities for retired members to keep in touch with former coworkers.*

To achieve an outstanding mature market program, combine features of both approaches, and refine them to match the needs and wants of niches within the mature market. The over-50 set includes all types of individuals in all types of financial situations. The broader your array of programs—and the more selectively targeted to primes, seniors, and elders—the more successful you'll be.

Suggestions for Building Relationships with Seniors and Elders

A strong mature market program combines programs and promotions targeting groups of individuals who share common characteristics. For your mature members with more leisure time—typically those in the senior and elder segments—we suggest the following.

Design an Outstanding Activities Club

Glance back at chapter 4 to review two examples of credit unions that have chosen to emphasize social activities for older members. As these examples showed, dynamic clubs do not come about without an upfront investment. Time and resources are necessary to get a club started, and to keep it going, a continued investment of energy is required.

From Dupaco Community Credit Union's experience we see that recruiting a retired individual to serve as senior program coordinator on a part-time basis can be an effective way to keep a program energized.

Figure 7.2 lists potential duties a senior program coordinator could perform, suggested by MEMBERS Prime Club. Consider creating such a position within your credit union.

In addition to recruiting a senior program coordinator, consider appointing a senior program advisory board. Draw upon your membership to choose four or five potential board members who represent a cross-section of your credit union's older membership. Ask them to meet quarterly to review existing services and member comments, and to suggest new services. Involving seniors in the planning,

Figure 7.2 Potential Duties of Senior Club Coordinator

- Explain benefits of your senior program to potential members, in person or on the telephone. Enroll these people in the program.
- Organize and coordinate club activities and outings. These could include educational seminars, local one-day trips, and special extended overnight trips.
- Monitor and obtain member perceptions toward credit union services and activities, and report these to credit union management. Assist in formal member research and follow-up projects.
- Answer or refer member questions regarding Social Security, Medicare, or other local services available to senior and retired members.
- Organize club members to perform volunteer projects for the credit union and community.
- Represent the credit union at local events with impact on older members.

implementation, and operation of your senior program will ensure that it reflects the needs and desires of the people it is formed to serve. Your club will benefit from their knowledge and expertise.

Tap into Senior Power

Your senior members represent a connection to the history and legacy of your credit union. Fairwinds Credit Union, mentioned earlier, offers an example of leveraging this fact to create dynamic programming.

In December 1998, Fairwinds kicked off the credit union's fiftieth anniversary celebration with a luncheon for Golden Anchor Club members. A 1948 film review, a reenactment of the charter application signing, and cash giveaways were part of the fun.

Suggestions for Building Relationships with Primes

Age 50 represents a gateway to a variety of transitions across a much-extended lifespan. Today's members approaching the second half of life are challenged to redefine what so many more "bonus years" of life will mean. You can take an active role in helping your prime members plan for retirement—or whatever comes next. People in the 50–64 age bracket need help preparing for an unchartered future.

Offer Prime Members Educational Opportunities

Credit unions have always taken pride in providing member education. Too often people focus exclusively on the financial aspects of retirement planning, overlooking the important lifestyle changes that will occur when they retire—or move into second or third careers. Equally important are maintaining good health, finding ways to fill newly available free time, and learning to keep a positive attitude when coping with change.

Life planning seminars reinforce the bond between members and your credit union.

Sponsoring life planning seminars provides your members with a valuable educational opportunity. It also gives them a chance to interact, share ideas, and enjoy social activities. Such activities reinforce the bond between members and your credit union. They also encourage older members to re-evaluate their relationships with the community at-large. How can they harness their energy and wisdom in service to the common good?

Lean on your CUSO

Credit Union Service Organizations (CUSOs) are becoming increasingly popular. They can empower your credit union to offer high-end investment products and services that regulations prohibit offering directly. If your credit union has a relationship with a CUSO, or with CUNA Mutual's MEMBERS Financial Services (formerly PLAN AMERICA®), your representatives from that organization are a friendly source of information on investments, retirement planning, and other financial management issues. Encourage them to write newsletter articles, prepare talks, or provide content for your web page.

WHAT'S NEXT FOR MATURE MARKETING?

Marketing to mature ages and life stages is about to undergo a dramatic change. Already, roughly 50 percent of the United States population is over 50 years old, according to *AgeWave* magazine. Those baby boomers who will dominate the prime segment by 2005 are transforming the transition to the "second half of life." As never before, tailoring your message to smaller and more specific target groups will pay off.

Boomers will have many needs and interests—but as always they will be self-focused in a way their parents were not. Marketing messages that match offerings to the interests and needs of specific life stages will be more likely to draw and hold boomers' attention than more unfocused mass messages. Credit unions have tremendous opportunity to serve boomer primes as they prepare for retirement and beyond, if they address them as the redefiners they are destined to be—thanks to the ongoing "longevity revolution."

Get ready for the party—the baby boom is coming! Boomers are fortunate to be experiencing their peak earning years in a time of prolonged prosperity. Many want to retire early and will have the money to do so. And as they have for every life stage, they will redefine what retirement means.

Many boomers delayed entry into working life to make time for a prolonged youth. Dropping out of college to travel the world or explore alternate lifestyles, they experienced unheard-of freedom to indulge their interests. Only grudgingly did many rein in their pursuit of self-fulfillment and apply their considerable energy to building careers and families.

For many boomers, the intervening years of intense work life and parenting have represented a compromise. They look forward to a retirement resembling their earlier, less-pressured lives. Self-fulfillment via education, travel, and community and family involvement is high on their wish list.

Implications for Credit Unions

The graying of the baby boom will not resemble anything we've seen to date. What are some implications for credit unions?

Still the "Me Generation"

Eddie and the Beaver may have turned 50, but they'll never stop being symbols of the baby boom. A cohort that grew up loved and indulged has developed into an unparalleled consumer culture. It's likely that boomers' appetites for credit products will not slack off as they age—rather, with time finally available for self-indulgence, the need for loans to finance recreational products and meaningful experiences will only increase. Credit unions can serve in several ways, both by providing loan products and by assisting members with wise financial planning.

Inheritance of Wealth

Not only is this cohort doing well in its peak earning years, it's in line for a potential windfall estimated to exceed $10 trillion. This will be the largest transfer of wealth ever to any one generation. One quarter of boomers are expected to inherit nest eggs totaling $50,000 or more. Boomers who are lucky enough to inherit money will need assistance in managing it. Others will need help building their own wealth through investments. Start positioning your credit union *now* to answer those needs.

You've Come a Long Way, Baby

Boomers helped generate a social revolution that included the dramatic influence of the women's liberation movement. Today large numbers of women are found well outside their traditional roles. One impact for financial institutions is that women today are actively involved in financial matters once left to husbands and fathers. This is quite different from the life experience of previous mature women. Whereas many of your senior and elder women members want and need financial education offered at a very basic level, women of the baby boom are more likely to find that approach patronizing and out-of-date.

Women today are actively involved in financial matters once left to husbands and fathers.

Boomer females have a dramatic impact on product and service purchases. They're responsible for the majority of leisure decisions. They influence matters involving children, family health and wellness, houses and careers. It was boomer women who put Bill Clinton in the White House. Isn't there a good possibility these women will respond to financial services programs and promotions tailored to their unique needs and viewpoints?

Over the next few years, watch your mature membership patterns change dramatically. It's estimated that every 7.7 seconds, since January 1996, a baby boomer has turned 50. Within another decade, a majority will have reached that milestone. Half of boomers are women. How will you serve this sizable niche?

Reinventing Retirement

The baby boom has already begun to reinvent the traditional transition from work to retirement. Most will be veterans of the already well-established shift from single-employer careers to a free-agent nation. Today's workers are finding themselves retooling at various times, shifting through as many as four to six disparate careers as their interests evolve.

As noted in chapter 1, life is beginning to be experienced as a cyclical rather than a linear pattern. Periods of education, work, and leisure can recur at various times. As these individuals approach retirement, they may find themselves in a "bridge" period that could last from five years to as many as twenty. During this period people slowly learn to redirect their energy. Periods of intense work may be punctuated by pauses for sabbaticals, family care, personal health problems, or shifts to part-time employment, before the individual finally moves to full retirement. Some may find ongoing roles as mentors in the workplace, never really considering themselves "jobless."

Your credit unions could be the beneficiary of the brainpower of these people. There are many ways to tap the talents of older adults. Consider offering seasonal or part-time positions to older people. Ask retired executives to serve on boards. Encourage mentorship between older and younger workers. Watch the benefits accrue in many ways.

Where Will the Growth Be?

To ensure a stable future for your credit union, you need new products in the pipeline. But "new" is a relative term.

At one end of the spectrum are products that are innovations that truly have never been seen before. Reverse mortgages and long-term care insurance are examples of products that didn't exist until the needs of the mature market called them into being.

Most new-product successes don't come from "completely new" products, however. Most new offerings are modifications or additions to existing categories of products. Bundling membership in the national "MEMBERS Prime Club" with seniors club membership is an example of altering an existing product to create a new offering.

Most new-product successes are modifications or additions to existing categories of products.

At the other end of the spectrum from "completely new" products are innovations that come from simply repositioning an existing product. When you package an existing product differently, distribute it in a new area, or promote it with a different positioning, you take an "old" product and in a way make it new again. Offering seniors club members a promotional rate on opening a grandchild's share account takes an ordinary savings product and gives it a promotable twist.

What trends ought the credit union marketer be aware of, to meet emerging demands with fresh products and services?

Lifelong Learning. School is no longer just for children. Businesspeople attend classes in record numbers, either to retool for career changes, or to fill in gaps missed by previous experience. Older people pursue learning for the simple love of it, giving rise to the thriving Elderhostel industry. The market for educational experiences just keeps on growing. Credit unions can capitalize on this trend by offering more educational seminars, on topics financial and otherwise. Don't over-

---

Keep Up With Trends

Dozens of publications forecast trends, among them the *Popcorn Report* and *American Demographics* magazine. Enter these names in your favorite search engine, or simply enter "trend forecasts" and follow the threads. You are likely to find a strong consensus about where the next successful business niches may emerge. Two major demographic shifts are noted to be underway: the aging of the baby boom, and immigration from other countries. The America of the future will be older and more ethnically diverse than we have seen to date.

---

look opportunities to celebrate your members' common bonds through other types of seminars, including community issues, history, culture, and family life skills.

Health. Good health in retirement is vital to maintaining a desirable quality of life. Support your members' quest for wellness with education, activities, and encouragement. Nutrition, physical fitness, stress management, and sports activities all offer program potential for credit unions.

Credit unions that offer membership in MEMBERS Prime Club should promote its special savings on pharmacy services, eyeglasses, contact lenses, and hearing aids. These are direct health benefits for members.

New Nests. Changes in life stage bring about changes in the home environment. The number of empty nest households will increase 19 percent in the next decade, as predicted in *AgeWave* magazine. As baby boomers swell this life stage, empty nests may become the nation's most common type of household.

Once the kids leave home, couples find they have more money to spend on their own interests. In general, empty-nesters often focus on remodeling to fit their new lifestyle. Kids' rooms mutate into dens, home offices, and health clubs. Kitchens and baths often need adaptations to help older people safely remain in their homes. As family units dissolve and recombine, the concept of "home" itself mutates. We buy larger homes to accommodate newly blended families, smaller homes when the kids have gone. We buy amenities like hot tubs because we've earned them; we buy home security systems to protect what we've earned.

For credit unions, the possibilities are huge. Use home products for premiums . . . promote home equity loans for home improvements . . . offer reverse mortgages.

Travel and Leisure. Baby boomers are fueling the trend toward major spending on travel, leisure, and recreation. True to their idealistic roots, boomers are particularly drawn toward activities that provide "meaningful experiences." That may mean recreation that enhances family togetherness, or travel to adventurous destinations, or purchase of recreational vehicles, boats, and vacation homes. With retirement comes the time, and often the financial resources, to finally indulge in the pleasure of leisure—attending a cooking school in Tuscany, or rafting in Timbuktu.

Kern Schools Federal Credit Union in Bakersfield, California, presents an example of a credit union accommodating this trend. A retired high school principal reports, "The credit union has helped provide opportunities for fun. I took out a loan for a trip to Europe. I went to England, Scotland, and Italy for three weeks—it was wonderful."

Expanding Internet Services. Any service that can be augmented with an Internet component should be explored. Retired members who travel frequently, or who move away from the community, are able to continue their relationship as credit union members easily, thanks to the Internet. The experience of Michigan State University Federal Credit Union offers an example. Michigan State University FCU recognized early on the importance of technology. The result is a very high level of service. About 17 percent of members live outside the state of Michigan. They use their personal computers or telephones to access services. Distant members are able to check balances, review account information, call up loan and mortgage calculators, even pay their bills.

Many financial institutions, credit unions among them, delayed launching online transaction centers while waiting out the Y2K "millennium bug" issue. With that in the past, online financial services are expected to skyrocket as technological convenience and consumer confidence in security rise.

> *Online financial services are expected to skyrocket as technological convenience and consumer confidence in security rise.*

Social Activism. Don't be surprised if a wave of aging baby boomer activists becomes a feature of the nightly news. Recall the depth of feeling catalyzed by the seminal events of this cohort's coming of age—the Kent State shootings and the Democratic Convention of 1968 among them. A generation that remembers itself as "young radicals" may use its newfound free time to embrace social causes. Ed Asner expresses it well: "Your legacy remains through the work you do for the collective good." Expect to see your newest senior citizens involved in all types of causes. Tap their power when there is an issue to which the credit union movement should lend its support.

Lending and Savings Options for Maturing Boomers

These are just a few of the lending and saving products baby boomers in their fifties are likely to want.

- Vehicle loans
- Credit cards
- Second-mortgage loans
- HELOCs
- Other loans
- Share draft accounts
- Share accounts
- Investment accounts

NEW MARKETING TO SERVE MATURES

To succeed in the new marketing of today requires a product that is demonstrably one notch better than similar offerings. But finding a dimension to improve upon can be difficult. Marketers are discovering that sometimes the difference that makes something "new and improved" isn't in the product at all, but in the story behind it.

We need only look at the basic convenience of a share draft book to observe the difficulty of standing out in the crowded financial services marketplace. Older individuals who shop around will most likely be offered a free checking or share draft account anywhere in town. Why should they choose a credit union account with you? The answer lies in the credit union difference itself. Being a member-owner instead of just another customer is a good reason to locate that account under the credit union roof.

The lesson for credit union marketers? The story behind credit unions sets us apart from all other financial institutions. Market it.

No Stereotypical Images, Please. It's certain tomorrow's matures will be vital and productive. In your marketing communications, depict them as they really are: involved in activities, pursuing their interests, socially interactive, busy conquering challenges. According to Jeff York at Vista Federal Credit Union, the credit union of Disney, the Walt Disney Company just hired a vice president of human resources who came out of retirement at age 68 to accept the position. "As the baby boom ages we're seeing brainpower that can run companies when they're older. We bring in the elders' experience and combine it with new ideas. It's going to be a good partnering opportunity. We don't want to see all that skill go unutilized," York says.

Increasing Ethnic Diversity. As "tomorrow" becomes "today" the mature population will reflect the wake-up news that America is becoming more ethnically diverse, as shown in figure 7.3. Mainstream America is continually absorbing

Figure 7.3 Today's Diverse Boomers Are Tomorrow's Matures

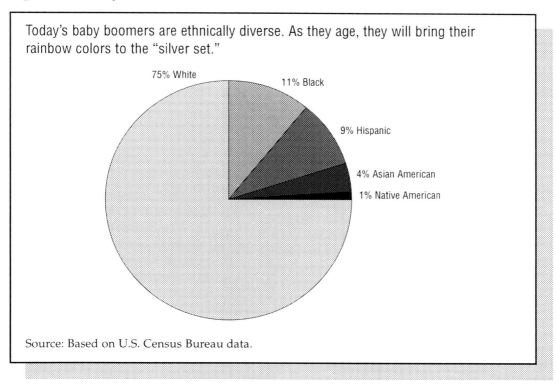

Today's baby boomers are ethnically diverse. As they age, they will bring their rainbow colors to the "silver set."

75% White
11% Black
9% Hispanic
4% Asian American
1% Native American

Source: Based on U.S. Census Bureau data.

elements of immigrant cultures into its fabric. The Hispanic, Black, and Asian-American communities are contributing their values to the new mix. Interestingly, these groups all place relatively greater value on the extended family than Anglo-American culture now does. Grandparents are especially revered in these cultures. The implication is that credit unions marketing to these cultural groups should emphasize eligibility of extended family members, uniting the whole family in credit union membership.

Because they have different backgrounds and lifestyles, ethnic groups tend to have distinct tastes in media. Your community may have radio stations that draw high listenership among cultural subgroups—a gospel radio station, perhaps, or a Hispanic pop station. Marketers know the importance of understanding customers' cultural values and media behavior. With this knowledge, effective messages can be developed that speak to specific cultures, or intentionally transcend them with universal messages.

"My Nonna Was a Great Storyteller"

Many ethnic groups have strong oral traditions and a reverence for older family members. Creative advertising featuring story-telling techniques and emphasizing elders will have natural appeal. Multicultural advertising is most effective when a mix of pictures, sounds, and words is combined. Take advantage of this by blending broadcast and print vehicles in your media plan.

Research indicates that individuals from ethnic populations have completed comparatively less formal education than white Americans, and a disproportionate number fall within lower income brackets. These observations hold significance for credit unions in two areas: our traditional affiliation with working folk, and our emphasis on education. Credit union marketing programs and promotions should reflect ethnic and generational diversity—so that our marketing reflects who we are and whom we serve.

AND THE PRIZE GOES TO . . .

The future belongs to those who practice relationship marketing. Simply put, relationship marketing is nurturing individual customers over time. When your oldest members were young, this is the way everyone did business. The local butcher knew Mrs. Green liked her roast trimmed lean and that Mrs. Marroni would complain if hers had no fat. The clerk at the neighborhood soda fountain knew to pour coffee for Mr. Vladyk and to draw a chocolate phosphate for his wife.

In the intervening years "progress" steered us away from that friendly style of business to the high-tech world we now counter with attempts to be "high touch."

As the mass consumer society attempts to steer itself back to a one-to-one style of doing business, information technology has been harnessed for mass customization. The result is a marketing industry that can deliver direct mail pieces personally addressed to you, but the result rarely feels like the relationship shoppers knew on yesteryear's Main Street. This type of marketing focuses only on gaining transactions, rather than creating a trusting long-term relationship.

> *The marketing industry can deliver direct mail pieces personally addressed to you, but the result rarely feels like the relationship shoppers knew on yesteryear's Main Street.*

True relationship marketing is the result of a two-way dialogue between individual customers and the organization. You must not only reach individuals with messages tailored to their interests—you must encourage feedback from them, and use it in meaningful ways. Increasingly efficient information technology makes this possible. A robust Marketing Customer Information File (MCIF) holds the key that unlocks the future of credit union marketing.

Lifetime Member Value. Each member represents not just today's transactions, but a lifelong stream of needs and purchases. On the surface this would seem to recommend that you direct your marketing attention to your younger members, who represent the greatest future stream. The younger market segments do indeed deserve to be the focus of a sizable share of your marketing resources. Even so, your older members, including the "new old" boomers, represent huge purchasing power—and huge needs. Not only will they influence development of a variety of credit union products and services, they'll be financing much of your activity with younger members. Additionally, they hold considerable influence among peers and extended family members when it comes to financial matters.

Considered in this light, your older members aren't just "silver"— they're gold.

Leveraging what we know about the mature market requires a clear understanding of who is eligible for membership, what they need, desire, and respond to, and how they'd like their credit union to help them with those needs and desires. Technological innovations, from more sophisticated MCIF database use to Internet service delivery, are essential components of mature marketing strategies. Just as important are great personal service, educational seminars, and social opportunities.

Combine what you've learned about niches within the mature market with what you know about the value of individual relationships with members, and the result is clear: dividends of member satisfaction, increased product usage, and loyalty.

CREDIT UNION ACTION STEPS

- Examine your credit union's charter. What categories of people aged 50–plus might be welcome as members? Your list might include older relatives of current members, older residents in the community, and/or retired employees of your SEG or other select group. Ask a member of senior management to review your list. Make sure you have an accurate understanding of your eligibility requirements affecting older adults.

- Explore ways to harvest the insights and benefit from the brainpower of your older members. Consider them as potential job candidates at every level. Invite them to participate on boards, committees, and in market research. Solicit feedback from them concerning your products, services, and policies—then find ways to put that information to work.

- Write a mature market tactical marketing plan. Revisit your thoughts from chapter 4's third Action Step. Ask a peer or manager to be your "planning buddy." Discuss your ideas for the marketing plan, and set a realistic date on when you will show this person a first draft.

GLOSSARY

Baby boomers Name associated with persons born between roughly 1946 and 1964. Name refers to a surge in the birth rate during time period after World War II.

Baby busters Another name associated with generation X. Refers to a slowdown in the birth rate (baby bust) that occurred after the baby boom.

Brand identity The associations and expectations a consumer thinks of when exposed to a name, or a logo, or a product. A brand brings the product or organization to life in the minds of the public—communicating and demonstrating its value.

Cohort A demographic generation. The term comes from the Latin cohors, the box-like fighting formation of a division in the Roman legions. Demographers frequently work with cohorts born in the same year.

Credit Union Service Organization (CUSO) A vehicle established by a credit union to market such products as annuities, insurance and mutual funds. Credit unions establish CUSOs because regulations prohibit us from marketing alternative financial products directly. A CUSO can offer the entire range of financial planning products, including mutual funds, annuities, insurance, health insurance, disability and long-term care, as well as investment advice, estate planning, and stock brokerage.

Debit cards A plastic card that performs transactions similar to a credit card, however, the funds are withdrawn from a member's share draft account.

Demographics The study of population patterns and growth over time.

E-commerce Conducting business transactions over networks and through computers. Narrowly defined, e-commerce is the buying and selling of goods and services, and the transfer of funds, through digital communications. However, e-commerce also includes all intercompany and intracompany functions (such as marketing, finance, manufacturing, selling, and negotiation) that enable commerce and use electronic mail, file transfer, fax, video conferencing, work flow, or interaction with a remote computer.

E-mail A system of worldwide electronic communication in which a computer user can compose a message at one terminal that is generated at the recipient's terminal.

Generational cohort A segment of the population sharing a range of birth years (typically 18- to 20-year spans) tied together by cultural, political, economic, social, and historical experiences shared as they were coming of age. Research indicates that our membership in a specific generational cohort is highly predictive of what we believe and how we buy.

Generation X Most popular name for persons born between 1965 and 1980. Name originated from Douglas Coupland's 1991 novel, *Generation X.* Age range of group varies depending on which source is used.

Generation Y Persons born after 1980.

Home financial services The ability to conduct financial transactions, such as transfering money between accounts, viewing statements, and performing other actions, via a personal computer.

Internet Worldwide network of computers that use the TCP/IP protocols to facilitate data transmission and exchange.

Kiosk A stand-alone structure that allows ATM transactions as well as the ability to view accounts, apply for loans, and conduct other financial business.

Latchkey kids Another name for generation X. Mothers who worked outside the home raised many in this generation. When the children returned home from school, they used their own "keys" to get into the house because both parents were usually at work.

Life stage Milestones in a person's life when the normal course of events is substantially altered and the most significant social relationships often change. Stages such as *empty nesting, retirement,* and *grandparenting* can be used to predict consumer needs, wants, and concerns.

Lifetime member value Each member represents not just today's transactions, but a lifelong stream of needs and purchases that add up to considerable purchasing power.

Market segmentation Classifying customers and potential customers by geography, demographic traits, spending habits, media preferences, lifestyles, and so on, to improve our ability to design products, services, and messages that match that segment's predicted needs and wants.

Marketing Customer Information File (MCIF) An MCIF enables your credit union to segment your membership into smaller subgroups of members that are similar demographically, geographically, and financially. The MCIF provides data preparation, query, analysis and reporting tools.

Mass media vehicles Print (newspapers, magazines), outdoor (billboards, transit), and broadcast (television, radio) media offering advertising time or space available for purchase that reaches a mass (i.e., undifferentiated) audience.

Matures People born before 1950.

McJobs College-educated persons going to work at McDonald's because they don't know what they want to do with their lives or because they can't find a job using their degree.

Media planning The process of deciding when, where, to whom, and how much you will advertise; what you hope to achieve; and what you intend to spend.

Online bill payment The ability to pay bills over the Internet via a personal computer.

Only financial institution (OFI) Term used when a person exclusively uses one financial institution for his or her monetary business.

Positioning A communication strategy that helps individuals identify what is unique about your organization. Positioning emphasizes those attributes in which you excel when compared to other competitors.

Primary Financial Institution (PFI) Individuals have many options for meeting their financial service needs. Most individuals, for convenience if nothing else, consolidate the majority of their financial relationships under one roof. This institution is known as their Primary Financial Institution, or PFI.

Relationship marketing Using marketing techniques to nurture long-term relationships with individual customers over time. Relationship marketing requires a two-way dialogue between individual customers and the organization.

Retail marketing The experience your customers receive from their interactions with your staff and your facility. Your retail marketing strategy reflects the choices you've made to distinguish your business from competitors.

Segmenting Process of dividing a credit union's membership into various groups to selectively target marketing efforts.

Select employee groups (SEGs) Companies and organizations that allow a credit union to offer its services to their employees as a benefit.

Silent generation People born before 1950. Also referred to as "matures."

Target marketing strategy A strategy calling for identification of subgroups that exhibit collections of traits which are predictive of the needs and desires of that unique segment.

Web page A block of data available on the World Wide Web. In the simplest case, a web page is a file written in HTML code, stored on the server. It may also refer to images that appear as part of the page when it is displayed by a web browser.

World Wide Web A collection of Internet sites that offer text, graphics, sound, and animation resources through the hypertext transfer protocol.

Yuffies Young urban failures.

BIBLIOGRAPHY

American Demographcs magazine. Also see *www.demographics.com.*

Constance Anderson, *Credit Union Marketing Handbook,* 1998 (CUNA & Affiliates).

Ken Dychtwald, *Age Wave: The Challenges and Opportunities of an Aging America,* 1988. Also Jeanne L. Engle, *50 More Successful Loan Marketing Ideas,* 1998 (CUNA & Affiliates).

Marketing by the Numbers, 1999 (CUNA & Affiliates).

Elizabeth Lipke, *An Intro to MCIF: How Marketing Customer Information Files Benefit Your Credit Union,* 1999 (CUNA & Affiliates).

Regis McKenna, *Relationship Marketing: Successful Strategies for the Age of the Customer,* 1991.

Susan Mitchell, *American Generations: Who They Are, How They Live, What They Think,* 2nd edition, 1998.

Don Peppers and Martha Rogers, *The One to One Future: Building Relationships One Customer at a Time,* 1993.

Tom Peters, *The Circle of Innovation: You Can't Shrink Your Way to Success,* 1997.

Robin Richmond, *Credit Union Branding: Winning Strategies for Marketers,* 1999 (CUNA & Affiliates).

Roper Starch Worldwide, *The Boomer Balancing Act: Baby Boomers Talk About Life and the American Dream,* 1996. Also see *www.roper.com.*

J. Walker Smith and Ann Clurman, *Rocking the Ages: The Yankelovich Report on Generational Marketing,* 1997. Also see *www.yankelovich.com.*

William Strauss and Neil Howe, *Generations: The History of America's Future, 1584–2069,* 1991.

William Strauss and Neil Howe, *The Fourth Turning: An American Prophecy*, 1997.

Richard D. Thau and Jay S. Heflin, eds., *Generations Apart: Xers vs Boomers vs The Elderly*, 1997.

Sarah White, *Complete Idiot's Guide to Marketing Basics*, 1997.

I N D E X

E

educational programs
    as advertising medium, 77
    for baby boomers, 109–10
    ideas for, 53
    lifelong learning and, 111–12
    life planning seminars, 107–8
elders, 7, 12–13
employer groups, advertising through, 76
employer-sponsored credit unions, 19
empty-nesters, 8, 112
Energy First Credit Union
    call center of, 85
    intranet advertising by, 75–76
    membership policy of, 95–96
    segmentation by, 97
ethics codes, 35, 36
ethnic diversity, 115–16
evaluation of advertising, 78
experiences, shared, 9

F

Fairwinds Credit Union, 103, 107
families, marketing to, 98, 116
field-of-membership policies, 94–96
Financial Network Investment
    Corporation, 55
financial planning, 23–24
financial programs, 105
first-class treatment, 37
Founders Federal Credit Union, 100
fraud, 24, 34
frontline staff
    appearance of, 79
    greeters, 83, 84
    training, 88, 89, 90

G

generational marketing
    defining segments, 5–13
    overview of, 1–2
    research and, 13–15
    segmentation and, 2–5

generations
    bonds within, 5
    segmentation by, 2–5
    shared experiences of, 9
G.I. generation, 12–13
grandparenthood, 8
greeters, 83, 84

H

health activities, 112
household information, 96

I

implementation strategies, 54–57
indirect research, 34–35
inheritances, 109
innovation, 111
insurance, 53
Internet
    as advertising medium, 76–77
    services on, 87, 113
    use by matures, 102–4
intranets, 76

J

joint club activities, 98

K

Kern Schools Federal Credit Union, 113

L

late adults, 7, 11–12
lending services, 20, 52–53
lifelong learning, 111–12
life planning seminars, 107–8
life stages, 7–9, 99
lifetime members, 117–18
listening skills, 89
loans, 20, 52–53
lobby displays, 82
long-range plans, 41

M

marketing. *See* generational marketing; research; retail marketing; segmentation; strategic marketing
marketing code of ethics, 35, *36*
marketing customer information files (MCIFs)
    application examples, 33
    capabilities of, 13–14
    household information in, 96
    relationship marketing and, 117
    use in sample promotions, 71
marketing plans
    long-range, 41
    strategic marketing and, 30–32
    writing, 57
    See also media planning
mass markets, 3–4
mass media advertising, 72, 73–74
matures
    differences among, 6, 7–9
    economic strength of, 18, 21
    importance of, 15, 16
    membership decline among, 19–20
    research about, 33–38
    retail marketing approaches for, 80–84
    segmentation of, 7, *13*
    stereotypes of, 17, 115
    targeting messages for, 96–102
    targeting services for, 21–26, 52–54
media planning
    assessing, 70–72
    basics of, 72
    efficiency in, 77–78
    objectives of, *63*
    requirements for, 56
    samples of, 67–70
    See also advertising
membership declines, 19–20
membership policies, 94–96
Members Prime Club, 55, 112
members, regaining, 54
message distribution strategies, 61–62. *See also* advertising

Michigan State University Federal Credit Union, 113
middle adults, 7, 9–11
missions and objectives, 30
multicultural advertising, 116

N

National Credit Union Brand Campaign, 51
new products, 111
newsletters, 77, 78, 100, *101*
nonmembers, marketing to, 38, 62

O

objectives
    in marketing plans, 30
    for media planning, *63*
    for promotions, 62–67
once a member, always a member, 16
one-to-one relationships, 42, 58
online financial services, 76–77, 102–4, 113
online security, 76

P

peer generations, 5–6
performance benchmarks, 32
personal services, *53*
planning. *See* marketing plans
positioning, 50–51
positive images, 99–100
Prestige Club, 82–83
pricing strategies, 40
primary financial institution status, 15, 25
primes, 9–11
Prime Time Club, 44–46, 89
Prime Time Profiles, 100, *101*
print collateral, *73*
print media, *73*
products, innovative, 111
profitability, 4
promotions
    examples of, 62–67
    sample media plans for, 67–70
    strategies for, 52–54

Q

qualitative research, 34
quantitative research, 34

R

redefiners, 10–11
relationship marketing, 107–8, 116–17
research
    planning and, 32–41, 77–78
    target marketing and, 13–15
retail marketing
    approaches to matures, 80–84
    convenience and, 86–88
    design and, 84–86, 87–88
    importance of, 79–80, 90
retirement
    baby boomers' desires for, 109, 110–11
    as life stage, 8
    membership declines and, 19
    planning for, 23–24

S

savings services, 53, 54
Seaboard Credit Union, 14, 34, 81–83
security, 85
segmentation
    evolution of, 2–5
    by generation, 5–13
seminars, 24, 107–8. *See also* educational
    programs
senior club coordinators, 106
seniors, 11–12
shared experiences, 9
simplicity, 37
singlehood, 8
situational analyses, 30–31
social activism, 113–14
social events, 44–45, 47–48, 105
Springtimers Club, 100
staff training, 88, 89, 90
standards of conduct, *36*

stereotypes, 17, 115
strategic marketing
    overview of, 30–32
    planning and, 41
    research and, 32–41
supertellers, 83
surveys, 33, 34, 75

T

tactical marketing
    examples of, 43–49
    implementation strategies, 54–57
    selecting approaches to, 49–54
targeted direct mail, 72
target marketing
    costs of, 4–5
    defined, 2
    planning for, 29–30
    research and, 13–15
    strategic planning for, 30–32
telemarketing, 74–75
telephone surveys, 34
television, 17, 73–74
training, 88, 89, 90
travel loans, 113
travel programs, *53*
trends, 112

V

V.I.P. Club, 46–49
Vista Federal Credit Union, 33, 41, 84

W

women
    of baby boom generation, 109–10
    as percentage of matures, 27
    services for, 25–26
workplace communications, 75–76

X

Xtra Advantage Club, 82

Marketing Across the Generations: Youth, Ages 0–19, #22900-JK1

Today's children and teenagers possess spending—and saving—power unparalleled in previous generations. Marketing to this group produces high-revenue, long-term relationships with low-risk members. This handbook, part of a four-part series, covers:

- designing effective products and promotions for the material generation;
- communicating effectively without falling into the "cool" trap;
- developing saving clubs, youth branches, and education programs;
- managing the transition from youth to adult member;
- measuring the effectiveness of your youth marketing efforts.

Short "Snapshots" describe exemplary youth marketing programs, and "Credit Union Action Steps" at the end of each chapter offer suggestions to put the strategies presented in the handbook to work at your credit union.

136 pages $29.95   2000

Marketing Across the Generations: Generation X, Ages 20–35, #22899-JK1

For many credit unions, identifying with generation X has become a critical factor as they make their long-range plans and position themselves for the twenty-first century. This handbook is one in a four-part series devoted to marketing to various age groups. It explores numerous issues relating to the generation X market segment.

This handbook helps credit unions develop programs targeted to generation X members ages twenty to thirty-five. It includes educational and informational programs as well as services that will attract these members. The handbook also provides methods for communicating with generation X and case studies of successful marketing. It also covers:

- age ranges used in defining generation X;
- characteristics, statistical, and demographic information;
- specific marketing issues and practical ways to reach gen Xers;
- E-commerce, Internet, and other technologies;
- the values and appeal of credit unions to generation X;
- the future forecast for generation X.

114 pages $29.95   2000

Marketing Across the Generations: Baby Boomers, Ages 35–53, #22898-JK1

Boomers are a large, diverse, and profitable market segment for credit unions. This handbook—one in a series of four—helps you understand how 76 million baby boomers are pioneering an extended midlife passage that will redefine how marketers answer their financial needs. The handbook also includes information on

- examining which credit union products offer the greatest appeal to baby boomers, and why;
- developing promotional and product ideas for the boomer market;
- providing additional services for individuals approaching their golden years;
- realizing the promotional and cross-selling opportunities of the Internet;
- assisting baby boomers with their saving, investing, and retirement planning needs;
- offering and marketing mortgage loan programs;
- becoming a one-stop financial center for boomer members.

"Credit Union Action Steps" help you put plans into action. Examples from experienced, frontline marketers illustrate promotional strategies that appeal to boomers. While difficult to pigeonhole, baby boomers represent an upscale, high-interest-paying market segment. The handbook helps you serve this profitable group.

120 pages $29.95   2000

Credit Union Marketing Handbook, #21253-JK1

Effective marketing powers successful organizations. Because of the special relationship credit unions have with members, marketing to both current and potential members is especially critical. You'll learn how to: develop marketing strategies for new and existing products, use distribution systems—both direct and indirect—effectively, use advertising, public relations, and sales promotion, develop pricing strategies to ensure growth while fulfilling your mission, formulate marketing objectives and goals, project sales, calculate the return on a marketing investment to track results, develop and manage the marketing process, and write a marketing plan. The appendix includes a marketing plan format.

166 pages $29.95   1998

Credit Union Political Action Handbook, #21305-JK1

Helps guide your credit union in effective political action at local, state, and national levels. Everyone who has the responsibility for safeguarding the future of our credit unions should read this handbook. This includes directors, volunteers, managers, marketers, and staff who handle communications, legislative, or political activities. Beginning with an introduction to the political process, the handbook rapidly moves to describe credit unions in relation to politics, elections, and legislation. It provides case studies in the areas of political process and lobbying. It will help your credit union create and maintain a consistent political presence, rather than rallying efforts only in time of crisis.

109 pages $29.95   1998

Security and Fraud Prevention Handbook for Tellers, #21252-JK1

Explores security concerns relevant to tellers. Useful for other frontline staff like member representatives. Can serve as a template to assist in training and writing policies. Beginning with an overview of security issues, it covers cash handling, counterfeiting, money laundering, check fraud, scams affecting members, internal security, and robbery and other emergencies. Chapters contain real-life examples and self-test activities. A great companion to the *Credit Union Teller Handbook #765.*

144 pages $29.95   1998

Credit Union Supervisory Committee Handbook, #763-JK1
Second Edition

Helps committee members succeed by giving them information on supervisory committee profile qualifications; makeup of the committee; removal from the committee; legal considerations; insurance protection; conflict of interest; duties and responsibilities; supervisory committee relationships—with members, directors, other committee members, management and staff, external and internal auditors, and your regulatory agency.

130 pages $14.95   1997

Credit Union Teller Handbook, #22823-JK1
Third Edition

Helps tellers and member service representatives get started and succeed, and also provides an excellent foundation for advanced training. Includes orientation to credit union uniqueness, teller's role and descriptions of duties and responsibilities, management expectations, policies and procedures, suggestions for handling emergency situations. Self assessments and checklists help reinforce key concepts and identify growth opportunities.

93 pages $24.95   1999

Volunteers and Lending, #21222-JK1

Offers a contemporary view of lending trends, committee roles, and the issues facing credit union lenders. Looks at the market forces that are causing credit committees to change, be replaced, or be eliminated entirely. Even though committees are changing, directors and volunteers still have responsibility for sound lending policies and practices. These important duties are outlined, with information and guidelines provided for various positions.

112 pages $29.95   1998

Managing Staff Recruitment: How to Hire the Best and the Brightest, #22258-JK1

Covers relevant employment laws, policies and procedures, job advertisements, preliminary screening, interviewing, and final selection. Also covers:

- understanding today's employment environment;
- attracting skilled people;
- recruiting techniques;
- identifying qualified candidates;
- interviewing effectively;
- providing employee orientation.

Your employees are your most valuable resource. *Managing Staff Recruitment* helps you retain a dedicated, long-term work force. Includes sample job application, interview guide, self-evaluation, job descriptions, and more!

181 pages $34.95   1999

Catch Members with the Net: A Guide to Maximizing Web Site Effectiveness, #22261-JK1

This handbook discusses the history, rationale, and uses of a web site, and the key concerns of maintaining and analyzing web site effectiveness. Includes:

- basic web site design;
- security and legal issues;
- keeping your content and design fresh;
- tracking your web site's effectiveness;
- marketing your site.

Also included are sample web sites, basic HTML instruction, a sample worksheet, and checklists. Web sites are becoming an integral part of credit union operations and marketing efforts. Learn how to create an effective site for your credit union!

150 pages $34.95   1999

Technocasting for Credit Unions: Identifying Tomorrow's Technology Needs Today, #22260-JK1

Discover the most compelling technology options available in the financial industry today, and learn how to take a systematic approach for your credit union technology decisions. Topics include:

- forecasting and planning for technology;
- new and upcoming technologies;
- possibilities and pitfalls of the World Wide Web;
- budgeting for and analyzing performance of technology;
- technology staffing and implementation;
- technology vendors.

Use *Technocasting for Credit Unions* as your credit union resource for making technology decisions. Feel confident that you're using technology to help members take control of their financial lives.

131 pages $34.95   1999

Online Laws and Regulations for Credit Unions: Internet Legal Implications, #22561-JK1

Explores the laws and regulations credit unions must follow in catching the growing wave of Internet commerce. Includes specific examples of how those regulations apply and the consequences of noncompliance. *Online Laws and Regulations* also covers:

- general legal principles;
- compliance issues;
- new accounts;
- lending over the Internet;
- electronic funds transfers;
- privacy and security concerns.

Includes a glossary of Internet terms and a reprint of an NCUA *Regulatory Alert* containing the NCUA's opinion on many of the compliance issues that arise in Internet transactions.

120 pages $34.95   1999

Credit Union Branding: Winning Strategies for Marketers, #22640-JK1

Provides the tools you need to meet the challenges of brand marketing. By giving brands distinctive qualities, brand marketers create loyalty for their products and services, and their credit unions. Provides a comprehensive background on the history, strategy, and opportunities of brand marketing. Includes:

- the lexicon of branding;
- functional and emotional benefits of brands;
- tactics for implementing a brand marketing program;
- trademark protection;
- brand consistency and revitalization;
- examples of great branding techniques.

Also included is information on the National Credit Union Brand Campaign. Learn how you can effectively manage your credit union brand!

122 pages $34.95   1999

Youth Financial Literacy: Preparing Youth for Financial Responsibility, #22646-JK1

Offers suggestions for developing formal financial curricula in schools; building community awareness of the need for financial education; and getting parents, educators, administrators, and students involved in the process. Youth Financial Literacy also covers

- developing highly focused relationships with youth;
- strengthening relationships with parents;
- providing training seminars for youth and parents;
- building rapport with school systems;
- becoming involved in community programs for youth;
- preparing Internet pages to educate youth;
- developing a youth program as part of the credit union's overall objectives and goals.

Illustrates how easy it is to develop savings, investment, lending, share draft, and other programs for youth, and provides case studies of specific credit unions' youth programs, classroom presentations, community activities, seminars, and special promotions.

147 pages $29.95   1999

An Intro to MCIF: How Marketing Customer Information Files Can Benefit Your Credit Union, #22624-JK1

The MCIF is a powerful marketing and technological tool. It can help your credit union increase its membership, increase members' use of the credit union's products and services, and improve the credit union's financial performance. This handbook will help credit unions understand the MCIF and use it effectively. Includes

- identifying MCIF alternatives;
- choosing the right MCIF alternatives;
- choosing the right MCIF solution for your credit union;
- understanding standard MCIF operations;
- learning how credit unions use MCIFs in marketing and strategic initiatives.

Also included are case studies, worksheets for comparing MCIF providers, and statistics from a survey of CUNA Marketing Council members on their use of MCIFs.

85 pages $34.95   1999

For more information on CUNA & Affiliates' products and services, check out our web site at *www.cuna.org*.

To place an order or
ask a question:

Call **1-800-356-8010, press 3**
(or dial ext. 4157)
7:30 a.m. to 6:00 p.m.
Monday–Friday, CST
Local calls 1-608-231-4157
TTY phone 1-800-356-8030

Fax 1-608-231-1869

Mail the order form to:
CUNA Customer Service
P.O. Box 333
Madison, WI 53701–0333

E-mail customerservice@cuna.com

CUNA & Affiliates Order Form

Ship to:

Credit union

Attention

Street address for shipping

City/State/Zip

Bill to:

Credit union

Attention   Title

Address

City/State/Zip

Phone   Ext. #

Fax

Payment method

☐ Credit unions in U.S.:
No need to prepay, we'll bill you for the total amount of your order.

☐ Individuals and International customers:
Must prepay in U.S. dollars.

Quantity	Stock Number	Description	Unit Price	Total

Subtotal: We'll calculate the freight and handling (plus sales tax if applicable).

Prices subject to change based on reprints and revisions.

Thank you for your order!